1/86   83/2406   R14,95
         808.9 Sav   uuf

         sp + sp

AFRICAN FIRESIDE TALES
PART I

AFRICAN FIRESIDE TALES
PART I

Xhosa • Matabele • Batswana

PHYLLIS SAVORY

HOWARD TIMMINS PUBLISHERS

Southern & East Africa · United Kingdom
North America · Australia · New Zealand

This book is copyright under the Berne Convention. No portion may be reproduced by any process without written permission. Inquiries should be made to the Publisher.

ISBN 0 86978 211 8

Published by Howard Timmins (Pty) Ltd. 1982
P.O. Box 94, Cape Town 8000, S.A.
Printed by Citadel Press, Lansdowne, Cape

CONTENTS

XHOSA

Foreword	9
Introduction	11
1. The Wicked Chieftainess	15
2. Nomathanga	22
3. The Bridegroom Snake	27
4. The Story of Nomehlomancinane	35
5. The Rule of the Ancestors	41
6. The Magic Fish Bones	46
7. Mbebe and His Wife	51
8. Mbulumakhasane	55
9. The Moon Girl Thangalimlibo	61
10. The Cow Chalaze	68
11. The Story of Mphephethwa	74
12. Kenkebe and the Indawas	81
13. The Magic Water-Pot	86
14. Sithembile and Her Snake	92

MATABELE

Foreword	105
Introduction	107
1. The Hare's Rope Trick	109
2. Which tells of how the Hippopotamus left the Forest Lands, and became a Creature of the Rivers and Lakes	115
3. The Honey-Guide's Revenge	122
4. The Death of the Chameleon	128

5. The Tale of Ngcede, the Spotted Cloud Warbler	132
6. Brother to the Rat	136
7. The Hare Outwits the Lion	141
8. The Downfall of Xoxo the Frog	147
9. The Hen and the Mongoose	153
10. A Race between the Tortoise and the Hare	157
11. The White Hornbill	161

BATSWANA

Foreword	169
Introduction	171
1. The Story of Puti, the Duiker	173
2. Tloding Pela	177
3. The Discovery of Fire	182
4. The Boy Ntabesana	188
5. Tswana	193
6. The Power of Tawana	199
7. The Crocodile Prince	205
8. The Silver Tree	213
9. Leruarua	217
10. Monyenyane and the Falcon	222
11. Selekane	226
12. The Lion and the Hare	232
13. Matong and the Big Black Ox	237

XHOSA

Illustrated by
GERALD BHENGU

FOREWORD

Phyllis Savory has done it again! She has collected a selection of stories from the folklore of the Xhosa people that are full of interest and very representative of the Xhosa type – for the Xhosa stories have a flavour all their own. They have three notable characteristics:

First of all their incidents have a logical sequence which is frequently absent from the majority of folk tales. Often grandmotherly tales wander along without apparent aim or purpose and depend for their interest on the word picture of the moment, without regard to the direction they are taking. Not so the Xhosa variety, which appear to have been more carefully composed with the eventual conclusion in view, and are built up in such a way that the end is almost inevitable.

Secondly they are told for the purpose of enforcing or, at any rate, supporting some point of family discipline or tribal custom. They uphold conduct that is for the good of society and the welfare of the community. They suggest that hardship, if stoically endured, is good for individual character.

Thirdly the actors in the stories lean heavily on magic to accomplish their designs. In fact stories that have no magic in them are few and far between in Xhosaland. Magic and make-belief are the stuff on which these stories rely for their popularity. Even bowls and spoons talk, and Zim, a hairy creature, uses the magical power of the nail of the little finger of his right hand to overcome his enemies. We read of the witchery that enabled an ugly monitor to impersonate a beautiful girl. We hear of a magic water pot that could turn clear water into either mellow beer or sweetest milk, and so it goes on. Magic meets one at every turn.

As in her previous collection, Phyllis Savory tells her stories in a language that is simple and direct and that skillfully preserves the idiom of the old grandparent who, of course, is the expert story teller in all the Bantu tribes.

As a kind of cherry on the top, Phyllis Savory has had these stories illustrated by Gerard Bhengu, a self-taught Zulu artist who, as might be expected, can depict the Bantu people with an accuracy unsurpassed by a European.

Grown up people as well as children, will find this book fascinating.

D. McK. Malcolm

INTRODUCTION TO THE XHOSA PEOPLE

The land inhabited by the Ama-Xhosa clans occupied the area of roughly 27 degrees to 29 degrees East latitude, by 32 degrees to 34 degrees South latitude in this great continent of Africa, which area covers approximately 100 miles square in extent.

Towards the middle of the 16th century the Xhosa clans lived as a united whole, being feared and respected far beyond their immediate surroundings. They are a dignified, bright and courageous people, free from self-consciousness and possessing steady and fearless eyes. They are looked upon as the aristocrats of the Bantu people.

As a tribe they are closely bound together and loyal to each other, and have a higher status than any of the other Bantu tribes. They were never brought to subjection by even Shaka, and have been conquered only by Europeans.

The name of the earliest known ancestor of these people was of the tribal name of M-'Nguni, and from this source the Aba-nguni people are descended. The next chief of importance was Xhosa, and it is by his name that the tribe is still known. He was the man who ruled at the advent of these people into their present surroundings.

During the Great Trek Southwards the Nguni clans broke off from the parent stem and, splitting still further, branched under their separate leaders into their present countries of Pondoland, Zululand and the Transkei in which latter place the Xhosa people are today.

Coming as they did from the North East of Central Africa, many of the characteristics of the Xhosa people are shared with the East African people. This can be traced in their Folk Tales.

As with most other Bantu tales, the ones in this collection are constructed so that part of one tale can be interchanged with and fitted into another, forming a new tale. As can be imagined, the expansion in this manner is endless.

One of the many examples that show early contact between the Ama-Xhosa and the North African people is the likeness of their present-day basketwork to that of the 18th dynasty of the Egyptians of 3 000 years ago, it having the same mode of patterns and shapes. Other modern Xhosa creations such as head-rests used as pillows, although not so elaborate as those of ancient Egypt, follow the same general character and design.

From farther north still came Jewish and Arab infusions, and from these sources can be traced the influences on their tales. Their religious sacrifices have clearly come to the Xhosa people through Asiatic sources – either through the Arabs or the Hamites (of which latter race the Bantu are an off-shoot), thus making them of Jewish origin.

The Xhosa sacrificial offerings are in many cases the same as those mentioned in the Old Testament – i.e. "fat from the intestines, with sweet-smelling herbs, and the breast reserved for the priest". The blood of the beast was also kept, but never eaten. Arab influences, on the other hand, can be traced from Somaliland down to the coast and on to Sofala.

Tales of "striking the water with a rod to make it part" (as in the Biblical tale of Moses and his people fleeing from the Egyptians), abound in these Bantu Folk Tales, and this is actually reputed to have happened at the banks of the Zambesi river when the Zulu chief Zwankendaba made his great trek over that big river on his way from the south to form the Angoni (Nguni) tribe on the east of Lake Nyasa in Central Africa.

From time to time during the middle of the 17th century, various Basuto clans sought refuge with the Xhosa people, so we have a Basuto name or tale creeping into the Xhosa Folk Tales. Also we find scattered Hottentot clans tacked onto the Xhosas, giving the light colour often to be found among them today.

As with nearly all the other Southern African tribes the Xhosas suffered from the cannibal invasions, bringing the wicked "Zim" or cannibal into a great number of their tales. This scourge of cannibalism was more often than not brought about as a result of starvation, and there are very few tribes indeed in whose Folk Tales you will not find this dreaded human creature mentioned.

It will be noticed that the snake fills a large role in some of the Xhosa Folk Tales (as it does also in the tales of various other Bantu tribes). This is understandably due to the fact that a number of Bantu people believed that their ancestors returned to earth in the form of various kinds of snakes, and therefore these creatures were revered and were never harmed. Often should a snake go into the hut of a Bantu man, he would not kill it, but would vacate the hut and wait patiently until "his ancestor" had departed of its own accord. This belief still holds among the unsophisticated.

Of course there are occasions where a European tale, told by a missionary of long ago, has been adopted and altered to fit the Bantu way of thinking, and is now looked upon as their own.

The Xhosa people have implicit belief in witches and wizards, although they do not fear them, and they have complete trust in the abilities of their own diviners. It is seldom that you will find a Xhosa tale without the inclusion of magic of some sort or kind, as will be realised on reading the following collection, which are very representative of their Folk Lore in general.

1

THE WICKED CHIEFTAINESS

Long long ago, in the days before animals and birds had lost their power of conversing with human beings, there lived a Xhosa chief, with his two wives.

No children had blessed his many years of marriage with his first wife, which had made the woman hard and bitter. Therefore, when the gentle young wife that he had lately married gave birth to a little son, the elder woman was so consumed with jealousy that she made plans to do away with the new-born babe. "For," she said to herself, "surely my husband will give all his love to the mother of his little son!"

She set her plans carefully and, before the mother had even seen her baby, she exchanged it with a new-born puppy, and hid the babe in an unused hut. This hut was known to be infested by a horde of vicious rats. "The rats will surely kill and eat the little one," said the wicked woman, "leaving no smear of blood upon my hands!"

As soon as she had fastened the door behind her the rats swarmed from their hiding places to devour whatever she had brought. But the little babe stretched out his hands as though he trusted them, and they halted. "So small and helpless!" they said one to the other, "and not unlike our own! We will care for him," and they snuggled round him.

Some time later the woman looked into the hut, hoping to find the baby dead. Instead she found that the rats were comforting him and trying to keep him warm. "Very well," she said, "I shall have the hut burnt down. That will kill you ALL, and still no smear of blood will be upon my hands." So she sent a messenger to fetch her husband, who was attending to his lands.

"Husband," she said on his arrival, "I beg you to burn down this old deserted hut, for the rats that live in it are destroying all our grain." The chief was angry at having been called unnecessarily, and in a hurry to return to his lands, but being ready always to humour his favourite wife, he set alight the old hut before he left.

But the rats had heard the woman's exclamations of annoyance, and also her plans to burn down the hut, so together they combined to drag the baby through the doorway as soon as she was out of sight, and they hastened with him to the sties where the chief kept his pigs.

"Sow," they said to a big black mother pig who was nursing her piglets in a secluded corner, "care for this little one for us, and hide him from one who would do him harm, for today we die!" and leaving the baby with the sow they rushed back to the hut where shortly after they were burnt to death.

"How is this?" the cruel wife said to the little mother a few days later, "your child grows more like a dog from day to day!" and the poor mother, nursing the puppy, hung her head in shame and despair, while she was publicly disgraced by all.

The sow was a kindly animal, and gave the same loving care to her human charge that she gave to her own babies, standing over him when he was hungry so that he might drink his fill – and he grew into a strong and chubby babe.

He was playing with his foster-brothers one day when the chief's foremost wife went to the pig-yard to see how her husband's pigs progressed. The sow saw her coming and tried, too late, to hide her charge behind her big ear – but the wicked woman saw him. "Eh!" cried the chief's wife in anger, "is that child STILL alive to plague me? I will have his foster-mother killed, and he will starve. Once more, no blood will be upon my hands!" and shaking her fist at them, she chuckled as she went to the chief.

"Husband," she said in her sweetest tones, "the big black sow is ready for killing, and it is long since you indulged me with my favourite food." So, to please his persistent wife the chief gave orders for the killing.

But fortunately the sow's big ears had heard her threat and, as soon as the woman was out of sight the kindly animal took her little charge to his father's favourite cow and said to her, "Cow, care for this little one for me, for my time has come to die!" and she went back to the pig-yard, where she was killed. Although the chieftainess pretended to enjoy the feast that followed, the wicked woman could not bring herself to eat the meat of the one who had nurtured the child she hated, so she went hungry.

By this time the little one could pull himself up onto his small sturdy legs, and was able to reach the milk with which the big red cow so willingly supplied him, and all went well for a time. However, one day the chieftainess passed through the cow-byre and saw the child playing at his foster-mother's side. The cow tried, too late, to hide him with her bulging bag; "What!" screamed the woman, "would you STILL escape me? I will have your second foster-mother killed, leaving *no one* to shelter you," and she went to her husband with the request for him to kill his favourite cow.

At first the chief refused, saying that she could have another from his herd, but she wept and pleaded with him saying that if he did not grant her wish, it would prove to her that he no longer loved her; so he finally gave instructions for her wish to be carried out.

But the cow had heard the woman's threat so she took the child now toddling by her side, far away from his father's home, to a pond by the river bank, where there lived an enormous frog. "Frog," said the cow, "care for this child for me, and guard him well, for my time has come to die!"

She left the boy with the kindly frog, who hid him under the shelter of an overhanging bank, where she fed him on all kinds of water-foods and fish, and where they lived together until her charge grew big and strong.

When the boy was ten years old his foster-mother said to him, "Child, I can do no more for you, and soon you will reach maturity. You must therefore seek the companionship of your kind, and fashion a life for yourself. But first I will search for some work for you to do."

The frog set off to carry out her promise, and soon heard of a powerful neighbouring chief who required a servant to cook the food for his reapers; and after thanking the good frog for her many years of kindness and protection, the boy set off to try his hand at cooking.

They called him "Mazinga" at his new home, and he was soon taken into their midst as one of their own, for he was a lovable child who did his work with a will.

Not long after his arrival, a deadly snake began to threaten the safety of all who travelled through the forest to their lands beyond. Cunningly it concealed itself along a branch of one of the trees beside the path each day, and struck downwards at those who passed below. Many of the good chief's subjects had died from its deadly bite.

The workers of the fields lived in continual terror of their lives, so one day their ruler called his people to him and offered the reward of a goodly piece of his kingdom and a chieftainship, to the one who rid the country

of the dreaded reptile. One man after another tried to win so large a prize; but one after another they were stricken down, before they even *saw* the snake.

One day the boy Mazinga was observed preparing a large pot of very liquid porridge. "Child why are you cooking now?" asked the villagers, "for have we not just eaten?"

"I go to reap our chief's reward!" was all that the boy would tell them, so they watched his preparations with interest. When the porridge was bubbling and boiling, he took a piece of cloth and making a pad from it, placed it upon his head. Then he called his friends to help him lift the heavy pot and place it on the pad. When this was done, he set off towards the forest without another word.

The villagers were curious to see what he had in mind, so they followed him at a distance. He had hardly more than reached the forest edge when, passing beneath a spreading tree, the vicious snake struck; but instead of fixing its poison-fangs in his scalp as it had done to victims in the past, it struck deep into the scalding porridge and, completely blinded, fell writhing to the ground. "Ah!" exlaimed those who followed, hastening forward to kill the snake, "the boy well deserves our chief's reward, for he has sharper wits than we!"

There was happiness and feasting when the news spread around the countryside that the dreaded snake was dead, and the chief fulfilled his promise by building a kraal for his clever young servant, and making him ruler of all the land as far as he could see on every side.

After many months had passed, a neighbouring chief and his wife paid a visit to Mazinga's former master. Before leaving they asked to see the young man whose clever trick had rid the country of the dreaded snake, for his fame had spread far and wide. So the young chief was sent for.

"Mai!" exclaimed the visiting chief's wife on seeing Mazinga, "this might be YOU, my husband, when you were young and brave. Who are your people, Little Chief?"

Mazinga assured her that he had no people, but had been reared by a kindly frog that lived under a bank at the river near by. "What!" laughed the man and wife together, "a FROG, you say? Let us see this 'wonder frog'!" So Mazinga took the couple to the pond by the river and called out the old frog that had cared for him.

"Yes," said the frog, after they had asked her if she had reared the boy, "a big red cow with liquid eyes brought him to me from over the yonder hills," and she pointed to where the questioner's home lay. "She told me to care for him 'for' she said, 'my time has come to die'. Ask the cattle who shared her byre, if you want to know more – *they* might know," and she hopped under the bank where her home was, and they saw her no more.

"Come, we will ask the cows," said the old man. So the three of them climbed over the hill to the old stone byre where the cows were kept. "Yes," said an old and scraggy cow, "Well I remember sharing my mother's bag with a human child – until a hard-faced woman had my mother killed."

"Cow, from whence did the child come?" asked the man and the woman together.

"Ask at the sty of the sow who brought him," replied the cow as she turned her back on them and began to chew her cud. "The pigs might know."

They found an old boar who was toothless with age, flapping his ears as he dozed. "Grandfather pig," they asked, "do you know of a child who was nursed by a sow?"

A far-away look came into the old boar's eyes as he answered, "Yes, so soft and small! He would push us aside till he found his place, as our mother suckled us all."

"But from whence did he come?" the wife asked urgently.

"Ask at the home of the rats who brought him," grunted the old boar, and he turned over to continue his sleep. "THEY might know."

"We will ask the rats in the tumbled down hut," said the old man excitedly, and they made their way to the hut where the grain was once stored. As they unfastened the door there was a scurry of rats in all directions. But one grizzled old rat seemed too feeble to move, and they went to where he lay in the centre of the hut. "Don't bother to kill me," he moaned, "for my days are almost done."

"Rat, do you remember a human babe whom your people gave to a mother sow?" asked the wife, with tears running down her cheeks.

"Not I," the old rat squeaked, "but often my grandmother told me of . . ." and he seemed to be lapsing into unconciousness.

"Rat, RAT!" almost screamed the chief's wife, "THINK BACK! *What did she tell?*"

The rat recovered with a start. "Of how she alone of the troupe had escaped from the burning hut . . . after they had given the chief's new-born son to a sow!" He lapsed into unconciousness again, and when they turned him over to thank him, they found that he was dead.

"Yes, that was the time," cried the chief's wife, beside herself with excitement, "that our baby son was spirited away, and replaced with a new-born dog."

No further proof was necessary, and the couple embraced Mazinga, after which the chief went to his first wife's hut and dragged the guilty woman out. The proof against her was too great for denial, and she ended by confessing to everything, whereupon he banished her forever from his kingdom and, with his gentle wife and his newly found son, lived to a ripe old age in happiness and contentment.

2

NOMATHANGA

In a remote boulder-strewn valley in the heart of Xhosaland, there lived among the rocks near a little gurgling stream, a dreaded "Zim" or ogre, and his only child. The Zim was a great big hairy creature who was feared by all the neighbouring villagers, for not only did he devour their cattle when he could drive them undetected from the river where they watered, but word went round that children too, often provided a tasty morsel for his meals.

All sought the refuge of their huts when he ranged abroad, for his strength lay in his right-hand little-finger nail which, apart from being the length of a man's arm, was curved like a sickle-blade, and was even sharper. Those who crossed his path or thwarted him, were mown down by a mighty sweep of this dreadful weapon.

However, there is good in even the worst us, and this particular Zim was by no means an exception, for he loved his little five year old son as he loved nothing else on earth. He grieved that there was no small sister or brother to act as playmate to him, and day by day he watched the little fellow wandering lonely and forlorn around their solitary hut – until one day, feeling lonelier than usual the boy approached his father and said, "Baba*, must I *always* live alone with you?"

"No, my son," the Zim replied, feeling that he could delay his plan no longer, "your loneliness has caused me much distress. Have patience until tomorrow, for then I will go to fetch a wife for you from the village over the hill. But this will require both stealth and cunning, for if the villagers catch me at my theft, their very numbers might prove too many for my magic nail. What then will happen if I die?"

"If you should die, my father," answered his little son with courage, "I will go to the village and avenge your death! See, I too, am growing a sickle-nail!" and he proudly showed his father his *own* sprouting little-finger nail.

An evil chuckle escaped his father's lips, and on the following morning

*Father.

he set out with a big bag slung over his shoulder to fulfil his promise to his son.

As soon as the chosen village came into view he hid amongst the aloes and boulders on the hillside until he saw the men go out with their spears and hunting dogs, followed a little later by the women with hoes upon their shoulders, to till the mealie lands.

"Ah!" he said to himself, "easier than I thought; there are only little children left." And he walked boldly into the village.

Catching sight of a plump little girl about four years old he seized and popped her, amid the screams and shrieks of her companions, into his big skin bag – and by the time the dreadful news had reached the mothers on the lands, the Zim and his load were lost to sight and well on their way back to the monster's home.

There was great sadness and distress as the news of her kidnapping spread round the countryside, for all were certain that little Nomathanga* had been killed and eaten. But there was joy and laughter for the little Zim when his father put down his load and untied the cord that fastened the mouth of the bag. "Wow!" he cried, his eyes round with wonder and excitement; "this is indeed a beautiful one! Is she to be my very own?"

"Yes, your very own!" smiled the father, delighted to see his boy's pleasure at his gift. "Look after her well, my son, for her value is that of many cows!"

Her tears were quickly dried as the boy brought his treasures and laid them down before her. Soon she was eating and smiling as they made a fuss of her. The little Zim laughed with pleasure when she told them her name, "for," he said, "she is surely as round and beautiful as a pumpkin could ever be!"

Day by day passed, then week by week, and these two little children grew more and more devoted to one another. Never were there angry words; and never were they apart as they hunted small fieldmice, modelled tiny clay oxen, and did all the things that small Black children do. The tumbling waters of the stream drew them to it, and they laughed and splashed in its alluring pools.

Now it happened that one day the women of the village from which Nomathanga had been stolen, set out from home to look for thatching

*Little Pumpkin.

grass with which to mend their huts; but suitable grass was scarce that year, and they wandered farther than usual in their search for it.

As they rested beneath a tree in the midday heat, they heard childish laughter and fun. "No-one lives amongst these rocks and boulders," exclaimed one of the women, "whose voices can those be?" They crept noiselessly towards the stream, and looking down they saw Nomathanga and the little Zim bathing and splashing one another in the shallows beneath a tiny gurgling waterfall: "Nomathanga lives! Nomathanga lives!" they whispered excitedly, hardly able to contain their joy. "She whom we looked upon as dead, is here! We must go and fetch our warriors to rescue her!"

They lost no time in returning to the village, where they spread the glad tidings. The following day plans were discussed, and their chief decided that the young men in full war dress would go to rescue Nomathanga from the Zim. So down the hillside the youths ran, shouting, flourishing their spears, head feathers flying and their monkey-tail kilts swinging; and as they approached the Zim's stronghold they chanted,

"PHUMA NOMATHANGA!" (Come forth, Nomathanga!)

"HLALA NOMATHANGA!" (Stay here, Nomathanga!) growled the Zim.

"PHUMA NOMATHANGA!" repeated the men, coming nearer.

"HLALA NOMATHANGA!" chorused the Zim and his little son together.

"PHUMA NOMATHANGA!" the young braves shouted for the third time. Then the Zim leapt forward to meet them, and with his great sickle-nail he mowed them all down "r-weeee!"

When the warriors failed to return to the village, a band of older men was sent to find them. They too, charged down the hillside in full war dress shouting, flourishing their spears, head feathers flying and monkey-tail kilts swinging, while they too chanted as they approached the Zim's stronghold,

"PHUMA NOMATHANGA!"

"HLALA NOMATHANGA!" growled the Zim.

"PHUMA NOMATHANGA!" from the men, coming nearer.

"HLALA NOMATHANGA!" chorused the Zim and his little son.

"PHUMA NOMATHANGA!" shouted the warriors for the third time. Then the Zim leapt forward and "r-weeee!" the sickle nail mowed them

down – but not ALL of them this time; the last of the warriors managed to cut off the terrible little-finger nail with his spear before it reached him and, deprived of its power, the Zim fell down dead.

This remaining warrior then hastened back to the village to report the result of the battle to his chief, and a third party of older braves set out to rescue little Nomathanga. As they drew near to the scene of the battle they chanted,

"PHUMA NOMATHANGA!" But the little Zim put his arm around his tiny playfellow and pushed her behind him lisping.

"SLALA NOMATHANGA!"

"PHUMA NOMATHANGA!" shouted the warriors once more, drawing nearer.

"SLALA NOMATHANGA!" the little Zim lisped again, guarding her against them with his body; then he ran forward and, imitating his father tried to mow them down with his tiny little-finger nail. But his nail was soft and weak, and the men easily cut it off after which the little Zim too, fell down dead.

The warriors then picked up Nomathanga and carried her back in triumph to her mother, but although there was great rejoicing in the village because they had found their "Little Pumpkin", and also because of their relief that the country need no longer live in dread of the terrible Zim and his son, Nomathanga wept bitter tears, because she had grown to love her ugly "lord and master" with all her little heart, and she refused to be comforted for many, many days.

3

THE BRIDEGROOM SNAKE

Mavile was a scheming old man who was blessed with two lovely daughters of marriageable age and, with an eye to a good business deal in the shape of a handsome lobola or "bride-price" for these valuable possessions, he visited the neighbouring villages with this thought uppermost in his mind – listening to the gossip at each place.

Before long he reached a village where he learned from the people that they were in search of a wife for their chief. He pricked up his ears, for this particular chief, he was told, was indeed a dearly loved and powerful ruler, whose people were prepared to pay a goodly price for a fitting bride. He hastily returned to his home where he told his daughters that it was his wish to offer one of them as bride to this great chief.

"I, Father, as the elder, have the foremost claim," promptly broke in the bold and arrogant Mpunzikazi. "*I* will be the wife of this Noble One." Her sister said nothing, for she was a quiet and unassuming child.

Without delay the father sent a messenger to the home of the would-be bridegroom with the necessary betrothal gifts, and before long the marriage day was arranged and the father set about collecting a splendid retinue to escort his daughter to her new home. But to his intense surprise and great annoyance she defied him on this, the usual marriage custom, by saying, "I will go alone to my wedding feast!" And nothing that he could say or do would persuade this bold, self-willed girl to have a single retainer to accompany her upon her marriage journey.

Many were the heads that were shaken in disapproval as she left, unaccompanied, for her new home, and many were the mutterings that ill-fortune would surely pursue one who wantonly broke the tribal customs to this extent.

Shortly after setting out, Mpunzikazi reached the first river on her journey, where upon the bank she saw a crippled woman vainly struggling to lift a heavy pot of water onto her head. "Daughter, help, oh! help me, for I am deformed," the woman called out after her as, ignoring the cripple's plight, the girl commenced to cross the water.

"What! help you and waste my time, when a bridegroom awaits me at the end of my journey?" called back Mpunzikazi as she hurried on.

"May your journey bring disaster in its train!" muttered the woman after her.

The day was hot, and when some farther distance had been covered, Mpunzikazi looked around for a shady tree beneath which to rest and shelter from the sun. Before long she saw one, but as she drew near to it she noticed an old, old woman sitting in its shade. She stopped in horror at the sight that met her eyes for, besides being very, very old, the woman was full of sores, her hair was matted with filth, and she was altogether a repulsive sight.

"Have pity on one as old as I!" the old crone whined as Mpunzikazi drew near to her. "It is long since I have been washed or cleaned, for I am too old and feeble to do these things myself. May blessings be upon your journey, if you will help me!"

"*What*! clean one as filthy and as loathsome as *you*?" the arrogant one scoffed. "What benefit would that be to me?" and she passed hurriedly on her way – but not too hurriedly to hear the old woman mutter, "There goes a 'bad one', but her sins will find her out!"

Soon she came to a mouse sitting bolt upright in the pathway. "Shall I show you the way?" it asked her; but she brushed it aside without bothering to answer.

Next she reached a fork in the path, and was uncertain which branch to take. With no one to guide her she took the well-worn one which led to a much used ford across the river near to her journey's end. Here she was addressed by a young girl who said, "Sister, where do you wish to go?"

"What is that to you?" asked the arrogant one, "and who are *you* that you should address me as your sister? Be careful of your tongue, for I am come to wed the one who rules this land!"

"In spite of what you say," advised the girl graciously, ignoring her rebuff, "listen to the advice that I would give to you. Do not enter the village on *this* side; go in the other way."

Thereupon Mpunzikazi, little realising that this was the chief's own sister who thus addressed her, told the girl to hold her tongue and, crossing the ford, walked straight into the village.

She was about to enter it when a frog barred her way and addressing her it said, "Mpunzikazi, when you prepare the food for your marriage feast, will you give me some of the delicacies to eat?"

"Get out of my sight!" the girl replied, kicking the little creature out of her way as she proceeded hastily into the village. There she was received with suspicion. "For," said the people one to another, "whoever heard of a father sending his daughter on her wedding trip without a bridal retinue?"

However, they offered her the ceremonial mat on which to sit, and she sat on it. When she had rested they gave her some red mabele grain to grind. "For," they told her, "The Great One is away, and he will expect to find his favourite food awaiting him on his return."

She ground the mabele coarsely (because at heart she was a lazy girl), and taking it to the new hut that had been prepared for her, she made it into a mabele-cake, and, having cooked it, she placed it by the dying fire, and went to sleep.

When midnight came she was awakened by a roaring wind that was like a mighty tornado blowing, and terror filled her heart as its force blew down the door that closed the entrance to her hut. Guided by her screams, a monstrous snake glided in and, rushing wildly round and round the floor, it halted by the pot of food. "So! She would give me RED-grain cake, would she?" hissed the mighty snake, "and dry at that!" Then he twined his sinuous coils around her arms and legs, and with his tail he thrashed her until her body was black and blue, and she fell senseless to the floor. After this, with a noise as though a second tornado had struck the hut, he left her.

In the early dawn the people of the village looked into the hut, and there they found Mpunzikazi, bruised and hardly conscious, on the floor where the snake had left her. "He has rejected yet another bride!" they whispered to one another and, jeering at her for the punishment that she had taken, they sent her back to her father with the request that their lord wished to have the younger daughter for his bride.

They gave no reason for this change of plan, and Mpunzikazi, humiliated and ashamed, held her tongue.

The old man now called together a large retinue to escort the younger sister, Mpunzanyana, to the bridegroom's home – and, surrounded by a fitting company, she was led away.

They followed the path that had been taken by her elder sister, and soon

reached the ford by the big river. There the bride was the first to see the crippled woman struggling on the bank to raise the water-pot upon her head; "Eh! Grandmother," she cried cheerfully, "why do you strain your old bones when your granddaughter is at hand?" and leaving the retinue she told them to wait for her while she carried the load to the crippled woman's home.

"Daughter of my daughter*" said the old woman gratefully, "may you be rewarded for your kindness. Your journey shall bear sweet fruit."

With a smile Mpunzanyana returned to the ford where she rejoined her retinue, and they continued on their way.

Soon a halt was called that all might rest, and making for the shade of the same large tree as the elder sister had, they found the same dirty old woman sitting propped against its trunk. "Maiden, have pity on one as old as I!" she whined as the bridal party approached her; "it is a long long time since I have been washed or cleaned, for I am too old and too feeble to do such things myself. May blessings be upon your journey, if you will but wash me!"

The others turned away in disgust at the revolting sight, but Mpunzanyana's heart was touched, and although she shuddered at the task ahead of her she smiled cheerfully as she answered, "Good-day, my Great-Grandmother! but where are those who should care for you in your old age? Come, I will soon make you feel a great deal better than you look." And taking a little gourd of water from the old woman's side, she proceeded to wash and tidy the poor soul. After this was done to her satisfaction, the girl used her own bridal comb to groom the filthy hair.

"May you be rewarded for your goodness!" crooned the old crone gratefully, "and may good fortune travel with you!" Thanking the old woman for her blessing Mpunzanyana rejoined her retinue, and once more they continued on their way.

Not long after this the same little mouse appeared in the pathway and, sitting up in front of her it said, "This is where your path divides – for better or for worse. Shall I tell you which branch to take?"

"Dear little mouse, how good you are!" replied Mpunzanyana. "We are strangers in this land, and will gladly follow your advice."

"Take the smaller path that leads to the unfrequented ford, and there

---

*A term of endearment.

listen to the words of one who would help you," cautioned the mouse, and they heeded his words.

At the edge of the water by the little ford they came upon a girl with a water-pot upon her head, who addressed Mpunzanyana pleasantly saying, "To where are you going, my sister?"

"I go with my bridal retinue to yonder village," smiled Mpunzanyana pointed to some huts ahead. "May we all find favour in your sight!"

"Take the advice of one who looks upon you with pity," said the girl kindly, "and approach the village from the *other* side." And they followed her advice.

As they were about to enter the village a similar frog to the one who had confronted her sister, jumped in front of Mpunzanyana. "Sister," it addressed her, "when you prepare the food for your marriage feast, will you give some of the delicacies to me?"

"Poor little frog! he *shall* have a change in his monotonous diet of ants and flies," she thought to herself. "Why *of course* you shall have a share of the feast, you strange little guest!" she answered it aloud.

"This is indeed kind of you," said the frog with gratitude. "You are generous besides being compassionate – and for the thoughtfulness that you have shown on this your wedding trip, you shall be rewarded. Be careful of what lies ahead of you, for trickery surrounds you as a test to prove your worth. The bridegroom that awaits you is an enormous snake!

"But if you will follow my instructions, you will subdue him and he will not wish to harm you. Therefore listen carefully to what I say, and great happiness will be yours. When you are greeted at the village and are offered the ceremonial mat on which to sit, tell them to bring you a new mat. When your hostess gives you red mabele grain to grind in preparation for your bridegroom's evening meal, refuse to grind the red grains – ask for white. When the grain is ready, make and bake a good mabele-cake and put it in an earthern pot, asking for amasi* to go with it.

"They will show you into a new hut that has been prepared for you, but you must refuse to sleep in it – ask for a different one. When you settle down to sleep, put the pot of mabele-cake and amasi at your head. Fear nothing, and whatever happens during the night, do not speak or move."

All these things Mpunzanyana did – following the frog's instructions

*Amasi – curdled milk.

with the greatest care, then she settled down to sleep. But not long had passed before she was awakened by a wild wind blowing – a veritable tornado that as before, blew down the door that closed the hut of the sleeping girl, and fanned the dying fire back to life. By its flickering flames she was horrified to see an enormous snake slithering in at the broken doorway. She almost screamed, but fortunately her throat seemed too paralysed to form a sound until, remembering the frog's warning, she calmed her fears.

Round and round the inside of the hut the fearsome reptile slithered until, reaching the head of the pallet on which she lay, it found its favourite food that Mpunzanyana had so carefully prepared. First it ate with great enjoyment then, breathing a contented sigh (which, to the terrified girl sounded like a mighty hiss) laid its head on her breast and slept.

But there was no sleep for Mpunzanyana, and her relief was beyond imagining when, as the first cock-crow ushered in the dawn, the mighty snake slid quietly out through the open door, and away . . .

"Ah!" said the people of the village, looking in at the now sleeping girl not long after. "The Great One has eaten! The Great One is pleased! Tonight he will return as one of us!" And they went away rejoicing.

Soon an old woman came to Mpunzanyana, "Child!" she cried, with tears of joy running down her withered cheeks, "did he speak to you?"

"No, my Mother," the girl answered. "He came with the roar of the four winds of heaven, but he left as the breath of a contented sigh."

The old woman knelt at the girl's feet and wept for happiness. "Tonight he will come again," she smiled as she got up and dried her eyes, "and your fears will pass."

True to the old woman's prophesy, that night as Mpunzanyana lay in growing terror as the hours passed, the wind arose once more; but this time it came as a gentle sighing, and as a caressing murmur, and into the hut there came a handsome man. Laying his head upon her breast he whispered, "My Beloved One, your kindness and your trust have restored my human shape to me!" and her heart was too full for her to answer him.

Far into the night he talked to Mpunzanyana of the trouble and the curse that had been laid upon his father's young and lovely wife – the mother who had borne him – and who, at the birth of her "snake-child" had been disgraced and shunned by all. "But," he ended, "her belief has always held that the time would come when the trust of such a one as you would end the curse, and so restore me both to my people and to her. Tomorrow I will re-instate her to the position that she held before the curse was laid upon her – the Mother Queen of all her people; the foremost wife of all."

It was a happy wedding that took place not so very long after this, and when the Wedding Party returned to the village of Mpunzanyana's father, they carried with them many noble presents, and the deep gratitude of all the people of the countryside for the long-awaited return to them, of their beloved lord.

4

THE STORY OF NOMEHLOMANCINANE*

In a small hut at the foot of a mountain there lived a cruel old giantess whose name was Nomehlomancinane, which means "she of the small eyes". Although she herself was a wicked cannibal, her little daughter Nomahamle was good and kind and tender-hearted.

On the other side of the mountain there lived the giantess's sister, with her three lovely daughters. Now, in spite of the fact that these three little girls were her nieces, wicked old "small eyes" longed to put their plump bodies into her enormous "stew-pot", and her daughter often heard her muttering to herself. "Wait until I can lay my hands on those little nieces of mine. They are so fat, besides being nice and soft for my sharp teeth!"

Tender-hearted little Nomahamle couldn't bear her mother's cruel ways and begged her not to talk of such wicked things. But to this her mother would reply. "It is only you, my child, that I could not kill, because you belong to me, and I love you; as for those fat little cousins of yours, why, they are just right to make a tasty stew for my dinner."

To be related, even distantly, to one who ate human flesh was considered a big disgrace in those parts, and the mother of the three little girls had kept this shocking family secret from them. So that when her daughters came to her one day with the request to visit their aunt and cousin over the mountain, she was at a loss to know what to do. She tried all manner of excuses to prevent them from carrying out their wish, but they cried and fretted to such an extent, that at last she agreed to their request.

Her greatest treasure was a magic bird and this, she felt might help to keep them safe – so, tucking it under her eldest daughter's clothing, told her never to let it leave them. She warned them that there were monsters and fierce wild animals on the mountain heights, so advised them to take the path that led *round* the mountain side. Then, collecting some green mealies for them to make umphako on the way, she sent them on their journey.

The three little girls set off in high spirits; at last, they thought, they would see those who *really* belonged to them – their own flesh and blood.

*No-me-hlo-ma-nci-na-ne.

But they had not travelled far when they met an old man who asked them where they were going, and to whom they belonged? "We are going to visit our aunt Nomehlomancinane, she of the small eyes, who lives on the other side of the mountain!" they replied excitedly.

"Eh!" replied the old man, "I pity you. Poor little children. Your aunt is a wicked giantess, and she will eat you this very night!"

"Surely," they said, one to the other, "such cannot be, or our mother would not have let us come!" and disbelieving the old man, they continued on their way.

When midday came the youngest one said tearfully, "Sisters, my legs are not as strong as yours, for I am younger. Let us rest and eat, for I can go no farther." They sat down under a tree to ease their limbs and satisfy their hunger – and while they were resting an old woman passed along the path.

"Where do you come from, children?" she asked, "and to where do you go?" And when they had told her she shook her grizzled old head sorrowfully and said, "Daughters of my daughter, return to your home before it is too late, for your wicked aunt over the mountain is a giantess, and will eat you before this day is done!"

But *still* the children did not believe what she told them, and the eldest answered. "But grandmother, why did our mother not stop us from coming on our journey? She said nothing – but gave us her magic bird and sent us on our way. Maybe her bird will look after us, for it is too late to return to our home before nightfall."

"Ah!" said the old woman, "your mother was too ashamed to let you know the truth. However, she has tried to help you, for this is Integu, and he will save you if you give him this magic corn to eat." She put her hand into a skin bag that hung round her neck and taking out a handful of corn, gave it to the eldest girl, "Give him this," she added and, mumbling a blessing over them, she sent them on their way.

As the sun sank over the foot of the mountain they came to a lonely hut on the very edge of a big forest – the last habitation in a lonely land. A little girl was playing in front of the hut, and as they approached her they called out happily. "Surely this must be our cousin!" But the child covered her face with her hands and wept when she heard who they were – the very relations whom her cruel mother wanted for her dinner!

"Oh! Cousins," she cried in distress, "what CAN I do to save you?

My mother is a merciless cannibal, and although you are her flesh and blood, she will most certainly eat you! Come, I will hide you all." She led them to a large corn basket behind the door and bade them get inside. "Quickly!" she added urgently, throwing in some food for them, "for I hear her returning from her hunt!" as a voice reached them calling: "Nomahamle, my child, have you swept the hut and fetched the water for me, as I asked you to do?" The three little sisters had reached their hiding place not a moment too soon, for following on the voice, there strode into the hut no other than the wicked giantess.

"Yes Mother," the child replied, "I have done all the tasks you set for me to do."

"Good child," said her mother approvingly, "that is why I love you as I do. But, my little girl," she went on, after a pause, raising her nose and sniffing the air, "there is a VERY nice smell in this little hut of mine today! Just the same as the smell of the blood that runs in my OWN veins!" and she smacked her lips as she continued, "What a delicious supper I shall have tonight!"

"Nonsense! my Mother," replied little Nomahamle, "whatever do you mean? There is no one here; your imagination is playing tricks on you. Knowing what you are, who do you think would *dream* of paying you a visit?"

The giantess' nose, however, guided her straight to the big grain basket and, opening the lid she looked inside. "Oh!" she repeated with joy on seeing the children, "*what* a delicious supper I most *surely* am going to have tonight!" and she pinched the plump little arms of the child nearest to her.

Leaving the children shivering with fear, she turned to sharpen her axe and to prepare her largest cooking pot in readiness for her "stew" while Nomahamle wept bitterly.

As soon as the fire was blazing, she approached the grain basket to catch the first of her nieces, but as she bent down and raised the lid, the little bird flew up into her face and sang,

> "It is a wonderful thing that you do, Nomehlomancinane;
>   You have killed so many, Nomehlomancinane –
> But still you need more, Nomehlomancinane;
>   Even your own relations, Nomehlomancinane –
> Tomorrow it will be your own child, Nomehlomancinane!"

The giantess was dumbfounded at the bird and its song, and was completely mesmerised by its magic powers. This gave the children their opportunity to escape, and they lost no time in scrambling from the big basket and, taking Nomahamle with them the four girls ran for their lives.

Before long the giantess recovered from her trance and, in great anger at, not only the loss of her supper, but of her beloved daughter as well, picked up her axe and hurried after the fleeing girls.

Before long she saw them in the distance, and soon caught up with their short legs – but just as she was about to lay hands on one of them, the bird Integu flew into her face again and sang his magic song:

> "It is a wonderful thing that you do, Nomehlomancinane;
>   You have killed so many, Nomehlomancinane –
> But still you need more, Nomehlomancinane;
>   Even your own relations, Nomehlomancinane –
> Tomorrow it will be your own child, Nomehlomancinane!"

Once more she was held under the spell of the magic bird, and again the children fled. But they were soon too tired to run any farther, so took refuge in the branches of a very tall tree – and there the giantess caught up with them.

More enraged than ever when she found that she could not climb up after them, she began to chop the tree down. The axe was sharp, and it was soon evident that the tree was about to fall, when Integu again came to their rescue. But this time, instead of mesmerising the wicked woman, he worked his magic on the tree itself, which immediately grew taller and all the chips flew back to their places in the trunk where she had chopped it, leaving not a sign that the axe had even touched the bark.

With many mutterings of anger, the cannibal woman began to chop anew – but being intent on her work she did not see a man approaching through the trees. It was the father of the three little girls on his way to his sister-in-law's home, hoping to overtake his daughters before they fell into her clutches.

Hearing the children's screams for help, and seeing what the giantess had in mind, the father soon realised their danger – so he crept up behind her as she chopped. Signalling the children not to draw her attention to him, he took a big stone and, with a well aimed throw, knocked her senseless to the ground. Then he took her axe, and with it he chopped the cruel woman's head off, saying as he did so, "That is the end of *your* wicked life!"

He took the four children home, where all welcomed the tender-hearted Nomahamle to live with them, and there the four little girls grew up together in great happiness.

5

THE RULE OF THE ANCESTORS

Mdinini and his wife were very poor; but although the husband had to work for their living, they could look back to times when there was no need for such toil – times when Mdinini's ancestors had ruled this land in which they lived, possessing great flocks and herds. Now, all that was left of their by-gone splendour was the ancestral wooden bowl and spoon in which his wife Nyengula daily prepared his midday meal of amasi.

It was a well known rule throughout the land that such a spoon and bowl were passed from father to son, and from son to son again. Such heirlooms should be used by none but their rightful owner, for this was "The Rule of the Ancestors", and none dared to disobey it.

Having no children to help them in their daily tasks, life was indeed hard for these two, so one day Mdinini said to Nyengula. "Wife, there is little to keep starvation from us; I must go and seek work to earn our living for a while, from the rich chief over the hills. When my term of service is completed, I will ask for payment in the form of fine young cows, that we may build up a herd once more.

"You must care for our home while I am gone, and whatever comes to pass, YOU MUST NOT USE MY ANCESTRAL BOWL AND SPOON! Never must you even touch them unless you wish to clean them, for as you know I, and only I may use them." After she had assured her husband that she would respect his wishes, he set off on his long journey to the home of the rich chief over the hills.

For a time Nyengula religiously obeyed her husband's orders. She swept their hut, she tilled their tiny garden, and kept everything in order ready for his return. But daily, as she cleaned and tidied all around her, the ancestral wooden bowl and spoon seemed to beckon to, and mock her from the wall on which they hung. At first she was afraid to even touch them lest something dreadful should befall her.

But it would never do, she thought, for her husband to find his precious possessions covered in dust on his return. So she carefully took them down one by one, and dusted them one day. Nothing happened; she looked to see if they had marked her hands perhaps – and was relieved to find them whole. "Just an ordinary old bowl and spoon after all!" she thought, as she hung them up again.

Day after day Mdinini's forefathers' possessions continued to tantalise and torment her, and the more she tried to put the matter from her mind, the greater became her desire to eat from the forbidden vessels – until at last she was tempted beyond endurance. She again took them from the peg on which they hung and, instead of returning them after their usual dusting, she placed the spoon inside the bowl, just as she had always done when preparing her husband's food. This done, she cooked the umphothulo* to eat with the amasi, and made all ready for her meal.

As she bent down to place the food in the bowl, she was startled to hear a voice come out of it which said, "Nyengula, if you wish to respect your husband's orders, do not put any food in me!" But Nyengula had by now firmly set her mind on carrying out her desire to eat from the forbidden bowl and spoon, so she answered scathingly. "What! you wooden bowl! Why should I not, when it is my wish to do so? and why should I obey a piece of wood? A human being carved you into what you are – and now you try to give a human being orders – I have never heard of such a thing!"

However, the woman felt slightly uncomfortable when the bowl answered her saying, "Those who play with fire are apt to get their fingers burnt!" But she told it angrily to hold its tongue, if it had one, and turned to lift down the skin bag that held the amasi, ready for her meal. She hesitated, however, when as she laid her hand upon it, the spoon said, "Nyengula, I heard your husband reminding you about the customs of this home, and also warning you not to use us – NOW what are you intending to do?"

But Nyengula only laughed as she replied, "This is a strange home indeed; a talking bowl, and a talking spoon! Whoever heard of such a thing? Hold your tongues, both of you! There is nobody here to see me so I will sit in the sun and eat amasi in YOU, bowl, and with YOU spoon."

Once more the bowl and spoon warned her – together this time they said, "Nyengula, for the last time, listen to our words of warning. In

---

*Stiff porridge made from mealie meal.

this home you know that it is against the custom for a woman to sit in the sun to eat her amasi!" But the stubborn woman refused to listen and, taking up the bowl of food she put the spoon into it and left the hut. She chose a nice sunny place and sitting down began her meal, muttering to herself as she did so. "Hmm, wonderful spoons and bowls in this home; they can talk!"

She put the first spoonful of the mixed porridge and amasi into her mouth; good! she was going to enjoy her forbidden meal in the sunshine. Then followed an equally successful second spoonful; she would teach the bowl and spoon not to call down threats upon her head. Indeed she would! But what had happened? As the third spoonful went into her mouth, the spoon stuck firmly. Nothing that she could do would loosen it – and the more she tried to pull it out, the farther down her throat it went until spluttering and crying for mercy, she sank exhausted to the ground.

"There you are!" laughed the bowl. "The Ancestors have got you as we said they would! You were too clever to be warned by a bowl and a spoon, so now you can find your own way out of your trouble."

The poor woman cried and moaned for help to no avail, and at last there came a crow to see what all the noise was about. Not being able to speak Nyengula pointed to the spoon in her mouth, trying to ask for help. But she got no sympathy from the heartless bird, who laughed at her distress and flew away croaking hoarsely. "It serves you right; it serves you right!"

A little later two doves flew by, and hearing her moans they asked what ailed her? Again she pointed to her mouth, and the birds had pity on her. Understanding the punishment that had befallen her, they asked what they could do to help? Should they call her husband? She nodded her head vigorously, pointing to the mountains in the distance, and the little doves flew away.

Before long they came to a group of workers hoeing in a field. "Maybe her husband is amongst them," said one dove to the other, so they perched upon a nearby tree, and together they began to sing,

> "Nyengula the wife, disobeyed her husband;
> Now she is caught by a wooden spoon.
> Mdinini, please come and release her!"

But no one took the slightest notice of either the birds or their song, so, sorrowfully shaking their heads, they continued their search. Time and again they stopped to sing their sad song wherever they saw workers hoeing in a field, until at last they came to the place over the hills where Mdinini had hired his services. This time, as they reached the end of the first line, they saw a man put down his hoe to listen – and when he had heard the second line he looked around to see who sang the song. Seeing the little doves, he understood their message so, leaving his work he hurried to his master and asked permission to return to his home.

All night long he travelled, and when in the morning he reached it, he found his disobedient wife kneeling down by the side of the hut in great distress. Her mouth was wide open, and from out of it the handle of his ancestors' wooden spoon protruded. "What ails you, wife?" he asked – but of course she could not tell him, and, with tears running down her cheeks, she pointed to her mouth.

"Ah!" exlaimed her husband, "did I not tell you never to use my ancestors' bowl and spoon? See what comes of your wilful disobedience! But I will try to save you," he continued, "for otherwise you will surely die." Reverently he then called upon the mercy of his ancestors, naming them one by one, and begging their forgiveness of his foolish wife.

When this was done he grasped the handle of the spoon and pulled it from her mouth, saying as it came away. "Wife, your disobedience will one day cause your death – as it would have done this time, had it not been for the kindness and mercy of our little friends the doves!" And in his gratitude he scattered corn for the birds.

Never again did Nyengula disobey her husband's wishes, for she had more than learned her lesson. And never again had the bowl or spoon cause to call down the ancestors' displeasure on any of Mdinini's household.

6

THE MAGIC FISH BONES

In a home of peace and contentment there lived a man and his wife, with Nondwe, their only child. Life was full of harmony and love as Nondwe happily accompanied her mother throughout the day, assisting her in all the daily tasks about the home.

Intense was the little girl's sorrow, therefore, when her mother died, and her father brought a step-mother into their home. The second wife was a cruel and wicked woman with a daughter of her own of Nondwe's age, whose name was Deliwe, and these two – mother and daughter – set about to make her life a misery to gentle Nondwe.

Her only comfort was her mother's dog which, since his mistress's death had never left Nondwe's side. Daily he licked away the tears that trickled down her cheeks as she herded her father's cows and goats on the lonely hillside, while the pampered Deliwe played at home.

The cruel step-mother had taken Nondwe's little stock of clothing one by one, to clothe her own daughter, and the sharpness of the winter winds had brought a greyness to her unprotected skin, while great cracks formed on her neglected, horny feet.

Thinner and thinner she grew as her tiny portion of stale porridge failed to satisfy her growing needs, and in the end she tied a cord around her waist – and this she drew in tighter day by day, to make the pangs of hunger seem less acute.

One day, while she watched her father's cattle drink at the river-side, and her usual hunger gripped her, she wept aloud. Her faithful dog, trying to forget his own hunger, licked her face to comfort her and as he did so, a voice that came from near at hand said: "Child, why do you cry?"

She looked around her in astonishment, for nowhere could she see a human shape. There was a splash in the water beneath the bank on which she sat, and she saw a fish with its head above the water gazing at her, and distinctly heard it repeat the words, "Child, why do you cry?"

She hastily dried her eyes and replied, "I cry from the weakness that my empty stomach brings to me. At home my dog and I go hungry, while others eat their fill."

"Wait!" said the fish, "that will *never* do." And he disappeared beneath the water to return after a short while with all kinds of river-food, and a juicy fish bone for the dog. When both had eaten their fill she thanked the fish for his kindness, and prepared to take the cattle home.

"One request before you go," the fish called after her, "*tell no one that I gave you food!*"

That night, when her step-mother handed her the leavings from Deliwe's platter, Nondwe shook her head and turned away saying, "I have no taste for food tonight." Then together she and her faithful dog sought comfort and warmth from the friendly goats.

Daily now at midday when the cattle drank, the fish brought food to satisfy their hunger – and Nondwe's body grew back to its former rounded shape and beauty.

There was someone, however, who was anything but pleased at this improvement in her looks; Deliwe's mother. And when Nondwe continued to refuse Deliwe's porridge scrapings, she asked her where she did her thieving?

"I do not thieve," replied Nondwe, but she could find no explanation that would satisfy the woman. Full of curiosity and suspicion, her stepmother set Deliwe to spy on her at a distance, to find out why it was that Nondwe and her dog never wanted food.

It was, therefore, not long before Deliwe saw the fish rise to the surface of the water at Nondwe's call, and return after a few minutes with as much food as she and her dog could eat.

Hastily Deliwe went back to tell her mother of what she had seen, whereupon the wicked woman made her plans. That night when Nondwe had once more refused to eat Deliwe's leavings she said, "Husband, I am ill; I must have a change of food. I can no longer eat what you provide – I MUST HAVE FISH. I beg of you to catch some for me tomorrow."

When early morning came, and before the others were awake, Nondwe hastily slipped down to the river and, calling the fish to the surface, told him of her step-mother's wish. "Ah!" said the fish sadly, "today I must die! But before that comes to pass, listen carefully to what I have to say. When my bones have been picked clean of flesh and thrown away, gather them up, for they will bring you peace and happiness." Then he sank out of sight and the waters closed over his head.

All through the morning the husband set his traps and snares among the reeds and water lilies at the river's edge; and no fish broke surface when Nondwe called to him at midday as the cattle drank. Once more she and her dog had to content themselves with Deliwe's leavings, or go supperless to bed each night.

Now, when the step-mother had feasted on the fish, she picked the bones and gave them to Deliwe to throw away. This her daughter did, casting them on a field nearby, where the chief's son tended his father's crops.

Before long the boy came upon the bones and stooped to move them from his path – but, to his great surprise they eluded him and he could not lay his hands upon them. "This is strange!" he said to himself, and tried again with *both* his hands, to lift them from the ground. Once more, as his fingers closed on them, they slipped from his grasp. They were like "quick-silver" in his hands; he could not hold them.

Soon he called the chief, his father. He too, and all his councillors tried to move the bones – but one by one they failed, until the chief exclaimed, "NO MAN amongst us can lift these magic bones. Now let the WOMEN try their skill! Send out word that the first among the maidens to bring them to me, shall marry the finder of these Magic Bones – my Royal Son."

Word was sent to all the girls both far and near, and they came in haste to try to win the honour of becoming the royal bride. One by one they tried to move the magic bones – and one by one they failed, turning away frustrated as the bones eluded them, until at last not a maid was left.

"Is there no one else?" asked the chief. "No maid in all my land who has not tried?"

There was a murmur around the circle of elders who watched, as a toothless old grandmother called out, "Nondwe is not here!"

"Then where *is* Nondwe?" asked the chief in angry tones, "and why did she not obey my orders?"

"She tends her father's goats and cows," answered the step-mother, "but let her be. She is a sorry sight, with her rags and sores, to come before her lord."

The chief, however, insisted saying, "I shall not rest until ALL my subjects have tried to solve this mystery." And he sent to the grazing lands for the little ill-used cattle-herd. Soon they brought her to join the gathering and, as she came in her tattered rags and skins, the people stood aside to let her pass between them to where her chief was waiting.

She stooped towards the bones – but before her hands had touched them, they sprang to meet them, and there in her hands they nestled, as she carried them proudly to her lord.

7

THE STORY OF MBEBE AND HIS WIFE

There are lazy people in all parts of the world, including Xhosaland, and in this country there once lived a man and his wife, in a little old hut. They had a comfortable home that was always neat and tidy, in spite of the fact that it had seen better days. Their one precious cow was always sleek and fat; their dogs were well cared for, and their fowls clucked contentedly around the yard, while Velaphi their happy baby girl was a joy to one and all.

All these things, and a great deal more besides, were the work of Nomdudo, Mbebe's diligent wife, who saw to the smooth running of the home while her lord and master tilled their two fields, and saw to the planting of the crops.

But Mbebe himself was as lazy as could be, and there were times when he would leave the crops to look after themselves for days on end and, putting the hoe over his shoulder as usual each morning when he left his home (so that his wife would think he was on business bent) would branch off the path when out of sight to visit his friends, where he would spend the days in idle gossip while the weeds grew, and grew and GREW.

And when he returned to Nomdudo at night time, to find a well-cooked supper waiting for him, he would scold her saying, "you lazy woman, don't you *ever* work while I am away seeing to the crops? Where is the sleeping mat to replace my old one? And where is the new beer pot of which I am in need?" And on and on he would grumble.

Patient Nomdudo bore these scoldings for a long time, but she finally could endure his unjust and railing tongue no longer, so answered angrily one night saying, "Husband, I have listened to your scoldings for the last time. Tomorrow you and I will change places for the day. *I* will do the hoeing, and *you* will care for the household work!"

The following morning Nomdudo took the hoe and set out for the lands, calling over her shoulder to Mbebe as she left, "Now, husband, please remember these things. First of all clean the hut and yard; the child must be fed and cared for – do not forget that she is young and will need many feeds throughout the day. The cow must be milked and grazed, and do not allow her to stray into our neighbour's fields; the dogs will steal the food if you do not satisfy their hunger. The milk must be set for curdling in the big imvaba* that hangs on the intsika† in the hut. The firewood is finished, and do not forget that *clean* water is required from the spring before you cook the evening meal, for I shall be hungry when I return, and shall look forward to some nicely cooked porridge on my arrival." Having completed her instructions, she left for the lands.

"Well," he thought, "I have all the day before me in which to do these simple tasks, so I can afford to do them at my leisure." But little Velaphi thought otherwise, for she had awakened with a healthy appetite, and raised her voice in no uncertain manner. "Bother the child!" he thought – however he quickly fed her, then, slinging her onto his back as Nomdudo did, he tied her tightly to him, so that he would have both hands free to do the work ahead.

Next he swept and cleaned the hut and yard, but the child was tied too tightly, and besides, she missed her mother's soothing songs and also the gentle rocking motion as she worked, so she showed her displeasure by grizzling throughout the day.

After the yard had been swept, Mbebe milked the cow who resented the unfamiliar hands, and missed Nomdudo's kindly voice so much, that half way through the milking she kicked the wooden bucket over and most of the milk was spilt. Being worried that there was so little milk left for curdling, he forgot to feed the cow, and left her tied up where she stood; forgetting also the dogs that waited expectantly around, he went into the hut and sat down.

"In truth," he said to himself, "that work has made me thirsty. I will quickly pay a visit to Malumi's hut, and see if his beer has ripened. One pull is all that I need to take the dryness from my tongue. I will soon be back."

But his brother's brew proved to be the best that his sister-in-law had ever made, and it was a very long time before he was able to drag himself back to his household chores. When he *did* return to his hut, he found the hungry dogs pulling the imvaba round the yard, trying to get at the curds inside it. However, it was fortunate that they had not found the pail half-

---

*Skin bag in which the milk is put for curding.
†The pole in the centre of the hut which keeps up the roof.

full of milk that he had forgotten to put into it for curdling. So he drove the dogs away, washed the imvaba and filled it with the milk that was left in the wooden pail. Then he turned his attention to the hungry fowls that had pecked a large hole in the storage bin, and were helping themselves to the grain.

It was nearly time to prepare the evening meal so, being short of firewood Mbebe decided to pull some faggots from the cowbyre to make a fire. This reminded him that the hungry cow was still tied up inside it where he had left her after milking. Well, he would quickly fetch the fresh water from the spring, he decided, and while it was heating on the fire, he would see to some food for her.

The hungry dogs, however, were sniffing round the intsika, on which hung the bag of curds so, taking little Velaphi from his back, he tied *her* to the pole, and put the milk-sack in her place upon his back for safety. He then hurried to the spring to fetch the water.

As he stooped to draw it up, the rope that secured the mouth of the bag came loose and the milk poured out of it all over his shoulder into the clear water of the spring, turning it a milky colour. The result of this was that with the clouded water and an empty milk-sack, he hastened home to set the water to boil before turning his attention to the cow.

"It is too late," he said to himself, "to take her out to graze. I will put her on the roof and let her eat the thatch. It is time Nomdudo renewed it." He placed some of the poles from her byre against the hut and, with a great deal of pulling and struggling, managed to persuade the ravenous creature onto the roof of the hut. "I must tie her up here somehow," he thought to himself as he put the thong by which she was secured, down through the thatch near the intsika pole that supported the roof. Once back inside the hut, he tied the thong to his leg, to make sure she did not stray.

This done, he settled down with a sigh of relief, to cook the evening meal in readiness for Nomdudo's return. As the water in the big pot began to boil, Mbebe hummed cheerfully to himself. "Surely," he thought "I have got everything right at last!"

But at that very moment the cow lost her footing on the sloping roof above, to fall dangling on the end of the thong that tied her. To make matters worse, her weight pulled Mbebe to the top of the tall intsika pole and there, by his leg, he hung!

Nomdudo returned from her hoeing as the cow was about to strangle herself as she swung on the end of her thong. "What *can* have happened here?" the woman wondered as she hastily cut through the thong with her hoe, and released the cow.

But little did Nomdudo realise that her husband was hanging at the top of the intsika pole inside the hut and, as she cut the thong, so he fell into the pot of boiling water and was killed.

"Look," said Nomdudo to those who gathered round to comfort her, as she pointed to her husband, "at the result of laziness!"

8

MBULUMAKHASANE

A trail of fire and death had followed in the wake of a band of fierce young warriors as they swept through the countryside; none had escaped their cruel spears until they came upon Nomaxhagwane, Hlakabulala's lovely adopted daughter. "Far too beautiful," they said as they stayed their spears, "to feed the vultures; we will take her to join the women of our lord. Go, maiden, and dress yourself in your wedding finery – for such beauty surely has a mate in view!"

Amidst her tears she gathered up her lovely beadwork, and under their stern eyes she donned it. True, she *had* made the pretty ornaments to adorn her beautiful body for her marriage feast; but now she would be given to somebody she did not love, for how could she hope to escape from these fierce and ruthless men?

They drove her on before them; up the winding pathway where she and her little friends had skipped and played from babyhood, then past the cattle track that had led the village herd to their drinking place. At the top of the hill she turned to look once more at her foster-parents' home. Up, up, up curled the smoke from their funeral pyre; they had indeed gone to join their ancestors, and she was now alone in the world.

On, on, on they drove her; but always she kept her mind on the direction of her foster-uncle's home for, although she had not seen him since she was a little child, she knew that she would find shelter and protection, could she only reach his home.

Black clouds gathered as they hastened on, and a burst of thunder rumbled. Just then one of the warriors pointed towards a bushy gully and addressing his companions said, "some straying cattle from a kraal we burnt at the beginning of our raid. Come, we will round them up and take them too, to our lord. We will leave the child to wait for our return. She dare not try to escape, for where will she find refuge? And should she try," he added darkly, "it will be the worse for her!"

Nomaxhegwane sank down gratefully on to the grass as the men spread out fanwise to gather in the scattered, unattended beasts. But no sooner had they gone some little distance from her then she began to look around her for somewhere to hide. The countryside was flat, with nothing but an ant-heap here and there to give her cover – there seemed to be no means of escape. Suddenly she fell into a well concealed ant-bear hole at the base of a small mound. "Ah," she thought, "I can hide myself in here," and she wormed her way along the burrow for some little distance.

It was dark inside the hole, and she felt that at any moment she might meet some fierce creature – the owner of the den; however, she decided that she would sooner this, than fall once more into the hands of those cruel men.

Clap upon clap of thunder now pealed above, and the warriors hastened back with the cattle. But before they had reached the spot where they had left Nomaxhegwane, great flashes of lightning split the skies, and the heavens opened as the rain teemed down in torrents removing any trace that the girl had left of the direction she had taken.

It was not long before the raiders had reached the spot where they had left her, and she heard the tramp of the beasts' hooves as they were driven over her hiding place. Wet and disgruntled, and mystified at her disappearance, her captors at length gave up the search and hastened on their homeward way.

Nomaxhegwane lay cold and sleepless for many hours, not daring to wriggle her way out in case the warriors were still looking for her, for she knew nothing of the storm that had raged above. But in the end she grew so cramped that she could stay there no longer and, squeezing her body backwards she gained the surface to see the early morning sunshine streaming over the horizon. She stretched her aching limbs and brushed the earth from her body, then sat on a little mound to work out a plan for finding her foster-uncle's home.

She turned with a start at the sound of a voice which appeared to come from beneath her saying: "Dear little maiden, how beautiful you are; and what lovely clothes you wear! To where are you journeying at this early hour, all alone?" and from a hole in the side of the mound on which she sat, there crept a long and scaly monitor. Slowly, as it fixed its glassy eyes upon her, her mind became confused, and soon she found herself telling her strange companion of her plight. She told it too, of the path she must find to lead her to her foster-uncle's home, and of the welcome that he would give her.

She tried to check the information that she was letting slip, but her tongue ran ahead of her thoughts, and she looked up with a start to find the strange creature stroking her arm in the most soothing manner, and gazing pleadingly up into her face. "Let me try on just ONE of your beautiful necklets," it begged.

"Poor little creature," thought Nomaxhegwane, as all her power of refusal seemed to leave her, "how sad to be both so naked and so ugly!" She hesitatingly untied one of the beaded ornaments from her neck and put it on the monitor's.

"Ah!" how beautiful," murmured the monitor. "Kind little maiden, GIVE ME MORE!" Then one by one it charmed the beaded finery off the now completely mesmerised girl, who was soon left with nothing on at all. The monitor finally pulled some dirty bits of spiderweb from the hole in the mound, and draping these over Nomaxhegwane told her to cover the remainder of her nakedness with mud.

During all this time the girl seemed to have had her reason sapped from her, but struggling to regain control of herself she cried in a panic at last, "Who *are* you that torments me thus?"

"Hush, hush! my child," the monitor soothed, "I am Mbulumakhasane, Queen of the Ant-heap, in my bridal robes, and I go to seek a husband. You are my khokhothi, my little slave. Come, we must hasten to find my foster-uncle's home!"

Slowly before her eyes the girl saw the scaly body increase in size and lose its reptile shape. Where claws had been came graceful hands; the face grew plump and round; and as the creature wrapped Nomaxhegwane's braided goatskin about her waist, the tail slowly shrank and almost disappeared. Nomaxhegwane tried to speak, but the wrong words rolled from her tongue. Soon she felt she *was* a slave, and obediently followed her mistress, doing as she was told.

Over the hills to the West they travelled, ever towards the setting sun, and they finally reached the country where her foster-uncle ruled as chief. There was much excitement when they reached his village and the foster-uncle heard the monitor's tale of woe. "Come in, my child, and welcome," he said, "but sad is the tale you bring. Who is that I see, standing outside our walls?" he added looking at the bedraggled figure of Nomaxhegwane, standing at the gateway of the village, "Fetch her in!"

"Let her be," the monitor replied impatiently. "She is my wilful little slave – send her to sleep with the others of her kind, among the cattle

and the goats." Nomaxhegwane was therefore sent to do menial work with the other village drudges, while Mbulumakhasane was fêted and lived the life of an honoured guest. "It is strange," said her foster-uncle to himself one day, "how a child can lose her looks on reaching maidenhood. My brother's foster-child gave promise of great beauty when she was young. There is now a strange look about her eyes that I cannot understand."

Daily the little village drudges were sent in the charge of an old old man to scare the birds from the ripening crops, and daily Nomaxhegwane was sent with them to earn her keep. During all this time her tongue had refused to speak the words she wished to say, until one day she begged the old man to guard the field for her while she bathed in the river nearby, and without waiting for a reply, she left him.

On this very day the chief's only son sat resting on the river bank, and as Nomaxhegwane entered the water he saw her beat the surface with her hands. And as she did so, the memory of the past came back to her in all its vividness. She saw the phantom village of her childhood appear above the glassy surface, and her foster-parents come out of it to welcome her, accompanied by all the friends she used to know. Gracefully she danced to meet them.

The chief's son gazed in bewilderment when he saw the little drudge join in the strange play that followed. In his mind he saw her clothed in all a highborn maiden's finery, and he gaped in astonishment as she danced with the ghostly men and maids. "Mai!" he exclaimed, "no slave or drudge could bear herself with such grace: surely she is a highborn maid!"

Never had he seen such beauty, and he knew that no one else would ever hold his heart. In haste he rushed forward and caught her before she could escape from him, and at his touch the spell that bound her broke. She told him then of how her foster-parents had been killed, and herself taken as a present for the raiders' chief; she told him of her escape down the ant-bear hole; and she told him too, of her meeting with the monitor who had charmed her looks and clothing from her by witchery.

He took her home and hid her in his sister's hut, while he told his father of how they had all been fooled. "Ah!" said the chief, "we will trick the trickster into betraying herself as the witch she is. We all know that scaly monitors like milk beyond all else, and we know, too, how they suck the cows at night, leaving empty bags at milking time – and there is yet *one more* thing we know of the wicked Mbulu; whatever else she may change by witchery, her scaly monitor's tail remains! Come, we will prove her by the 'milk-pit' test."

Immediately the villagers set to work to dig a pit, and into it poured quantities of milk. "Now," said the chief, "we will see if the mistress of the little drudge is guilty of witchery or not. Call the women from their huts, and bid them leap across the pit. No monitor's tail can resist the sight of milk. WATCH HER WELL!"

But when they called Mbulumakhasane to join the test she clasped her hands and moaned, "I am ill, I am ill! Let me rest."

"Ah!" the people whispered one to another, "she gives herself away. Force her from her bed, for her fear confirms her guilt!" and they dragged and pushed her to the pit. Slowly but surely down came the scaly reptile tail as it saw the milk as she stood trembling on the edge. When the people saw the tail they needed no further proof of her witchery and, into the pit they pushed the wicked Mbulumakhasane, while many willing hands filled in the earth on top of her.

The countryside rejoiced to see her meet the death she deserved so well, and fires were lit on the hilltops, while dancing and merrymaking celebrated the betrothal of Nomaxhegwane and the chief's son and heir.

9

THE MOON GIRL THANGALIMLIBO

Thangalimlibo was the daughter of a very poor man. He was so poor indeed, that his only possession besides his lovely daughter was a solitary cow, which supplied the two with milk. Thanga, as he affectionately called her, was given her name when she was left motherless shortly after birth, and her father had called her "The Little Pumpkin without a Stem".

For a short while her grandmother had cared for the newborn baby, but her father had soon taken her to his lonely hut in the hills, and she had grown to early womanhood under his loving care. But the little one was far from being an ordinary child for, from her earliest babyhood she refused to sleep at night time, preferring to sing and dance all through the silent hours, and she was at her happiest playing or working in the moonlight.

Her father indulged her in this whim because just before her death the mother had said, "Lungelo, my husband, you must never take our little one into the sunlight for, if you should do so you will lose her for ever". And after saying these words she had closed her eyes in peace.

Lungelo always carefully followed his dead wife's instruction in this matter, and little Thanga grew to be a very beautiful girl – so beautiful, in fact, that her fame spread far afield. Not only was she famed for her lovely looks, but for the magnificence of the crops she raised by her diligence in the hours when other folk rested and she tended her ageing father's fields, while the moon shed her pale light over the sleeping countryside. The few who saw her soon spread the fame of her beauty abroad, until everybody longed to see "The Moon Girl, Thangalimlibo".

Before long the only son of a far away chief heard of this "wondergirl" and felt that come what may, he must satisfy himself as to the truth of these reports. "Surely one of such beauty and diligence combined," he thought, "would be a fitting bride for the heir to a chieftainship as great as that of my father!"

He therefore dressed himself in his best visiting attire, and set out for Thanga's home; but realising that he had little hope of seeing her by daylight, he waited at the spring from which she nightly drew the water for her father's hut.

As the full moon climbed into a cloudless sky, the girl came singing happily down the path. She, too, was dressed in her prettiest attire, and her lovely body shone brightly in the moonlight, while her beads and bracelets glittered like precious stones set in silver, as they caught the moonbeams. Her face was radiant as the moon itself, and her teeth showed white as ivory as she shyly smiled to greet the good-looking stranger.

He caught his breath as she hesitated, not knowing what to say. But Thanga's heart was beating as fast as was his own, and no words were needed between them. The next move was to approach the maiden's father for his permission for them to meet; this the chief's son lost no time in doing, and seeing their radiant faces, Lungelo willingly gave his consent.

The chief's son went home with a happy heart to tell his own father of his good fortune, and of the beauty of his chosen bride. The chief, however, had heard of Thanga's strangeness, and was anything but pleased to think that he would have a daughter-in-law who spent her daylight hours in sleeping. But nothing other than their marriage would satisfy this love-sick youth, so when his mother realised his determination, she persuaded her husband to speak to Thanga's father with regard to the betrothal.

Before long everything was settled, and after a heavy bride-price had been paid, a wonderful moonlight wedding was arranged. When this had taken place, Thanga's father warned the bridegroom never to let his bride go out into the sunshine, telling him that if she did so, a great tragedy would befall him and he would lose her for ever.

Life passed happily for them both in her new home, and Thanga soon gained her mother-in-law's respect and affection for her diligence at night. "What matters," the old woman said to the chief, "if *I* gather the wood for the hut instead of our daughter? I am young at heart and strong. Think of the work she does in our lands at night time! I tell you we are fortunate in our son's choice." In face of such praise the chief was forced to hold his tongue, although these strange ways were a constant annoyance to him, and he did not believe that she would vanish if she went out in the sunlight.

All went well for a time and a strong, healthy son was born to Thanga, whom they named Dantalasele. One sunny day the fat and laughing baby was lying in his mother's lap inside the hut, when the chief called to Thanga to fetch some water from the spring. She looked around helplessly for her husband, hoping that he would help her; he had gone, she remembered, on a journey to a far away village – and she had seen her mother-in-law leave for the lands only a few minutes earlier with a hoe over her shoulder, so there could be no help from *her*. "My father," she said humbly, "may I be allowed to do your bidding when the sun has set?"

The old man told her angrily that he would beat her if she did not carry out his order, so with a heavy heart Thanga handed the baby to his nurse saying, "Child, care for Dantalasele while I am gone," and taking up a scoop, she put the water-gourd* upon her head and went out into the sunshine to carry out her father-in-law's command.

On arrival at the spring she looked nervously around her, then dipped the scoop into the water to fill the big gourd. But as she did so it slipped from her hand, and in the crystal-clear water she saw it sink down, down, until it was lost to sight.

"Now, how did it slip from my hand like that?" she muttered to herself. Trying to remedy the situation she took off her head-covering and, holding the four corners in one hand, bagged out the centre with the other. She then lowered it into the spring to draw the water up in that. It, too, slipped from her fingers, and she watched it follow the scoop out of sight.

"What clumsiness is this that makes my fingers all thumbs today?" she asked anxiously, and she took off her leather skirt, to make a bag with *that*, to draw the water up. It filled and billowed out; one draw should almost be enough, she thought – but when she made ready to pull it up, with a swirl and a tug it eluded her fingers, and it went down until it too, was lost to sight.

"How shall I clothe myself when I go home?" she thought. But there still remained the gourd, and maybe she could cover herself with some branches from the trees. So she dipped the gourd into the water; it would be a heavy weight for her to pull up alone, though if she but half filled it, she should manage.

*Dried shell of one of the pumpkin family.

The water began to trickle in, and she was almost ready to draw it up when an unseen force dragged it from her grasp. She bent down lower to catch it as it sank, and groped in the water to save it; but once her hand was below the surface, the water grasped her and would not let her go.

Into the depths the unseen power pulled her – and down, down, down it took her, until she reached the home of the Spirits of the Spring. There they bade her welcome, and there they kept her.

As time went on, and the mother did not return, Dantalasele became hungry and raised his voice in anguish, so the grandfather said to the nurse, "Child, go and see why the baby's mother is so long at the spring? Bid her feed him, then tell her to hurry home for I am hungry, and as yet no food has been cooked. The dark will soon be here."

The nurse put the baby on her back and hurried to the spring, but when she saw no sign of her mistress, she returned to the chief with the news that only Thanga's footprints were to be seen in the sand at the water's edge.

As time passed Dantalasele became more and more hungry, and soon the chief began to worry at what he had done – and matters did not improve when his wife came home from the fields. She scolded her husband for his stubbornness in going against his son's wishes, and slated him far into the night. They tried to feed the baby on curdled milk, but he spat it out and cried all the more; until, after many hours they all four fell into an exhausted sleep.

But soon his empty stomach awoke Dantalasele and he started to cry again, so the little nurse took him outside to comfort him. She walked towards the spring, but all along the path the baby cried and soon she began to sing in a tearful voice:

"Dantalasele is crying,
  The moon is shining;
The baby is crying!"

As her last words died on the stillness of the night, she reached the water's edge, and Thanga arose out of the depths. Stretching up her arms, she took the baby to her breast and let him drink his fill. She kept him with her while the nurse rested, then gave him back to the girl again and bade her take him home saying, "You must not tell those at home where I am, for the Spirits of the Underworld have claimed me, and they will not let me go."

When morning came little Dantalasele was laughing and full of happiness once more, and the grandparents could not understand the reason for it, although the nurse assured them that she had satisfied his hunger with the water from the spring.

Every night now while the old people slept, and in the day time too when she went to fetch water for the hut, the little nurse took the baby to his mother; and as she sang her song, Thanga rose from the water to feed Dantalasele as before. Again the mother would play with him before returning to the Underworld, and the grandparents continued to wonder at the happiness and contentment of the child.

After three days had passed the husband returned from his visit and the old man bowed his head in shame as he told his son that through his foolishness and disbelief, Thanga had disappeared. Although heartbroken and angry, the husband was relieved to find that at least his baby son was well and happy; but, refusing to believe the nurse's story about feeding him on water from the spring, he stealthily followed her when she crept from the hut that night.

With amazement and joy he saw Thanga rise from the water in response to the plaintive song, and he silently watched as the mother fed their little son. He dared not show himself for fear that she would disappear again so, with a troubled heart he presently returned to tell his mother what he had seen. "Wait until the moon is high tonight, my son," she advised, "then go and capture her by force."

When evening came, he tied a length of ox-hide thong beneath his arms then, asking his friends to hold the other end, hid with them among the reeds beside the spring.

It was a long wait before the nurse came down the path singing her sorrowful little song, and Thanga rose to the surface as she reached the water's edge. But this time she seemed uneasy, and looked around her nervously before she took the child. "Did no one come with you?" she asked the girl.

It was then that the husband rushed forward and caught Thanga, while his friends pulled with all their strength. Slowly the man and the struggling woman were pulled along the path; but to the fear of everyone, the water came with them, hissing and roaring as it foamed and swirled around them.

Higher and higher it rose until it seemed that the waves would engulf the very huts themselves; their mighty force then dragged the man and wife apart, leaving Dantalasele in his father's arms, while Thanga disappeared beneath the surface of the water once more.

*

Again the sorrowing husband went to the spring when all was still and quiet on the following night, and hopefully he waited at the water's edge calling his wife by name from time to time. Never a ripple disturbed the surface of the water until at last in despair he called loudly upon his ancestors to help him in his trouble.

As if in answer there emerged from the depths a cock, like no earthly bird that he had ever seen. It was larger than the cock we know, and it shone like the rising sun. "What disturbs you, young man?" it questioned kindly.

The chief's son related his troubles, telling the cock of how, through fear of her father-in-law, Thanga had disobeyed the orders of the underworld that had been laid down for her at birth, and of how, to punish her, the spirits had taken her to live with them at the bottom of the spring.

"All this I understand," said the cock kindly, nodding his head, "and I will help you. You are being punished for your father's foolish act, so your father must bear the costs. Go now, and fetch from his herd two fat oxen and a pitch black bull; such gifts will please the Spirits of the Spring, and they will restore your wife to you!"

The chief's son went home with a happy heart to do the cock's bidding and, as the sun sank below the horizon that evening he drove the three cattle to the spring. The golden cock met him at the water's edge and as the husband urged the two oxen into the water, the strange bird followed, proudly mounted on the big black bull.

There was silence for a long time after this, until at last the water parted and Thangalimlibo came out of it looking more beautiful than she had ever looked before, clothed in shining beads and garments from the underworld. Speechless with joy her husband took her hand and, as the dawn flushed the sky around them, they wandered back to their home, where she was never again asked to go out into the sunshine.

Then one by one the spring threw up the things that it had taken from her: the scoop, the head-covering, the skirt and the big gourd. There Thanga's mother-in-law found them when she went to draw the water in the evening, when the vapoury mists came down.

10

THE COW CHALAZE

In a lonely valley in Xhosaland there lived a husband and his wife with their two small sons, Siyoyo and Siyoyozane. But theirs was a far from happy home, for the father was a harsh and cruel man who ill-used his family to such an extent that at last, fearing for her very life, his wife ran away, to return to her father's home far away over the mountains.

It was a big sorrow to her to leave Siyoyo and Siyoyozane behind, but she felt that she would have paid with her life had she taken them with her. Maybe, she thought, her husband would be kinder to them if she were not there. He would certainly have followed her to get them back if she *had* taken them – for who else would herd his many cows? His cows, it seemed, were the only things he loved – and daily the two small boys were sent with them as soon as the dew was off the grass, to find luscious pastures for the herd.

There was no thought in the father's head for his son's well-being. "Take no food from home," was his golden rule. There were rats for those who took the trouble to catch them, he said, and isikonde* too, for the digging – when they were fortunate enough to find them. They could scratch for a living for themselves – or starve! But woe betide them if the cows were thin!

The gentle mother wept as she thought of their plight; no one now, to hide umphako, their favourite mealie food, under the flat rock where the cattle drank. No one to comfort them when they were beaten; she was sad indeed.

But if anything, the father grew more cruel to his children than before; and what with daily beatings besides starvation, the boys were soon in a sorry state – until one day Siyoyo said to Siyoyozane. "Brother, let us set out to look for our mother." And the smaller boy replied, "even the dangers of the road will be better than the life we lead. Why does our father give us life, only to do his best to starve us?"

"At least if we are not here, he cannot starve us!" remarked the elder

*Wild carrots.

boy with wisdom. "We will ride our favourite cow Chalaze; she is strong and young, besides which, she always does our bidding." So, leaving the rest of the herd grazing in the valley, they called the cow Chalaze and mounting her, rode in the direction of their mother's home.

After travelling for many miles they saw some huts in the distance and Chalaze, quickening her flagging footsteps bellowed long and loudly. Before she had ceased the two little boys added their voices to hers in answer singing plaintively,

"Kala, kala njalo, nkomo ka Baba;
Si funa Mama, nkomo ka Baba!"
(Cry, cry continually, Father's cow;
We want our Mother, Father's cow!)

Every Bantu person, man, woman and child learns their own cows' call so, hearing an unfamiliar beast raise her voice in anguish the villagers came out of their huts to investigate and, seeing the two children on a strange cow's back, asked them what they wanted.

All they wanted, the little boys said, was to know if their mother had passed that way several moons ago?

"Yes," replied the people on hearing her described, "but she continued on her way without stopping." They pointed along the path that disappeared over the hills ahead, and the boys urged the cow onwards.

On, on, on they encouraged their willing steed until, as the sun went down they reached a second group of huts. Once more Chalaze raised her voice and bellowed loudly, to ask her little masters the reason for this never-ending ride; and again they answered her question with their song, though wearily this time,

"Kala, kala njalo, nkomo ka Baba;
Si funa Mama, nkomo ka Baba!"

As on the previous occasion the villagers came out at the sound of the cow's unfamiliar voice, to ask the children their business. "Did our mother pass this way, many moons ago?" they asked tearfully, telling them her name.

"Go farther, go farther!" they advised the boys. "She went *that* way!"

and they pointed along the never-ending pathway over the hills. But the children were spent with hunger and weariness, so begged for shelter for the night for themselves and their cow. They were taken to an old deserted hut, while Chalaze was led to the cattle byre – but not a grain of food was offered to either the children or Chalaze.

They could not sleep for hunger, so in the early dawn they crept from the hut and mounting their good steed set off once more. From time to time Chalaze snatched a bite of grass as they went along, but never a taste of food passed the children's lips until, as the second evening approached Siyoyozane fell exhausted to the ground.

Gently the elder child picked him up and, with great difficulty climbed with him onto Chalaze's back, to continue along the footpath through the hills with his brother in his arms. But as night drew in upon them Siyoyo realized that he could last no longer, and was himself about to fall from exhaustion, when the brave cow stopped to low once more, for she had seen the light from a village just ahead. This time only Siyoyo answered her, in a very tearful voice,

"Kala, kala njalo, nkomo ka Baba;
Si funa Mama, nkomo ka Baba!"

But at last their journey was over, for willing hands came to lift the boys from the weary cow's back and carry them to a hut where a bright fire burned. And there, sitting opposite to the door, was the mother for whom they searched.

"Children!" she cried in astonishment, "how did you come all this long way alone?"

"Mother, it is food we want, not questions!" whimpered the elder boy, "and water for my brother."

After they were fed and rested and the morning had arrived, Chalaze was taken with the other cows to graze. But as she left the village those who drove her saw a cloud of dust approaching. "Surely that is their father, coming with his warriors to fetch his children home?" exclaimed the mother fearfully.

As the cloud drew nearer the elder boy looked frightened too, for he recognized his father's cows, which had been left grazing in the valley at home. But why had his father brought them all this long way? he wondered.

However, there was no cause for alarm, as no one was with the cows; they had followed the trail of the young cow Chalaze, and there was a general bellowing of recognition and joy when they saw her. This was wealth indeed for the mother and sons, and the three of them became of great account throughout the country, because of their riches.

*

For many years this fruitful herd multiplied – and when the boys had reached maturity the mother looked round for a suitable wife for each of them. Owing to her wealth she could afford to be careful in her choice and in due course, she found two sisters who were as good as they were diligent and beautiful to look upon, so the boys celebrated a double wedding.

To begin with, the bridegrooms lived in the village of their brides, but finally they wished to take them to their own ancestral home. So they loaded their possessions on to the back of their old cow Chalaze and, taking their mother with them, set off on their long journey.

Chalaze's steps were slow and faltering now, and nightfall found them far from any habitation. Deciding to sleep under the shelter of some trees at the forest edge they unloaded their goods from the old cow's back and, tying her to a nearby tree, settled down for the night.

They had not been asleep for very long when they were awakened by a mighty roar. "Thunder!" mumbled the younger brother drowsily.

"A lion, you mean!" corrected the elder one, sitting up and peering into the darkness. Nearer and nearer came the roars, until the earth shook with the reverberations.

Hastily they climbed into the branches of the tree above them – all, that is, except Siyoyo. Taking a blazing stick from the fire, he stood at the foot of the tree to await events. Soon the old cow took fright and, breaking the thong that tied her she plunged with a bellow of fear into the forest.

Intent on stalking the cow, the lion had not seen the elder boy, so all was soon confusion as Siyoyo ran to turn back Chalaze to the camp – and he heard the lion bounding through the bushes close behind him. Remembering the blazing stick he carried, he threw it into the thick dry grass through which he ran; dense smoke soon rose behind him, getting in the lion's eyes and the flames singeing his hairy coat. With a lion's inborn fear of fire, the great cat fled, while the cow and boy ran on . . . to find themselves, when daylight came, not far from the very home that they had left the day before!

At the edge of the forest the rest of the party searched in vain for the missing pair until, convinced that the lion had killed them both, they continued sadly on their way, eventually to reach the old ancestral home.

They found the father ill and decrepit and with nobody to care for him. They told him of everything that had happened, from the time the two small boys had run away from home, to the sorrowful ending of the night before. But their tears were turned to laughter shortly after when, looking along the pathway they saw an old cow approaching, with a man behind her, and heard her bellow long and loudly. Then in answer came Siyoyo's voice singing cheerfully,

"Kala, kala njalo, nkomo ka Baba;
Si funa Mama, nkomo ka Baba!"

There was merrymaking and gladness in the old home that night, and the sadness of the past was soon forgotten. The whole party continued to live with the old father and to care for him, and he was grateful for their kindness. His years of loneliness had mellowed him, and, in the years that were left, nothing pleased him more than to sit in the golden sunshine and watch his grandchildren playing at his side.

11

THE STORY OF MPHEPHETHWA

Mazwi and his wife lived near to the banks of a big river that flowed into the sea only a few miles away. Life passed happily enough for them in spite of their poverty, and the planting season gave promise of good rains ahead for their coming crops. Their small plot of land was radiant in the fair sunshine as Mazwi accompanied his young wife along the path that led to it, to turn the red earth ready for the planting.

Mazwi carried some food for the midday meal, while his wife shouldered a hoe; their tiny baby, strapped straddle-legged across her back, nodded his sleepy head as he was rocked by the motion of her stride.

There was very little shade in the neighbourhood of their lands, so the mother made a tent with her goat-skin robe and a few sticks, and there little Mphephethwa lay protected from the sun while his parents worked.

On the particular day of which I write, drugged and drowsy with the golden sunshine, the baby had fallen into a deep sleep. Presently there flew overhead a large sea-gull and his mate from the ocean nearby. "What strange object is *that?*" one gull asked the other, pointing with his beak in the direction of the little tent. "Let us alight and find out!" and they sailed silently down to the ground alongside of it.

Heads first on one side and then on the other, the birds drew nearer and nearer until, gaining courage, they at last looked inside. "How fat and round!" they said each to the other, "and *surely* good to eat. Let us take it home to our children." Between them they lifted little Mphephethwa and flew with him towards their nest near the sea-shore.

As they rose high into the sky Mphephethwa was awakened by such rough treatment and, seeing the earth so far beneath him began to scream and struggle with all his might. This was more than the big birds had expected, and certainly more than they could deal with, so they hastily bore him down to the sea-shore where, terrified by the noise he made, they left him to the mercies of the rising tide.

"My husband," said the wife to Mazwi, as she rested leaning on her hoe, "is that not our son I hear crying so bitterly in the distance? Has he been stolen from us while we worked?"

"Woman, get on with your hoeing!" her husband scolded her. "Those cries come from the village over the river yonder," pointing in the direction that the birds had taken. With a sigh of resignation his wife bent to her work once more; but she could not forget those terrified screams so, as soon as she had finished her hoeing, hurried to the little shelter she had made.

Sad indeed were the parents when they realised that they had been robbed of their little son, and the weeping mother reproached her grief-stricken husband all along the pathway to their home.

Down on the shore where the little one lay the waves lapped higher and higher as the tide rose, until finally they reached his fat little body. Just as this happened a big fish heard his pathetic cries and swam up on a wave to where he lay. "Come, little one," it said kindly, "I will take you to your mother." Opening its big mouth it swallowed him and, turning along the coast swam quickly in the direction of the baby's home.

Eventually they came to a river that poured itself into the sea and swimming up it, soon reached the bank near which Mazwi and his wife lived. Here the big fish put its head out of the water and, seeing a man about to cross to the opposite bank sang in a high-pitched voice,

> "I bring you sweet news, oh Man!
> For I carry a baby boy, oh Man!
> The sea-gulls stole him, oh Man,
> But I must ask for a reward, oh Man,
> Because one day he will be rich, oh Man!"

The man looked around him in astonishment because no one was in sight, and he was about to continue on his way when the fish brought forth from its mouth the very child for whom his people were searching so feverishly.

With a shout of joy he took the baby in his arms saying to the fish as he did so. "Pray, good fish, wait here while I call the child's parents, that they may reward you for your kindness."

But poor Mazwi was at once in difficulties; he was overjoyed at the return of his son but, having no possessions, he had no reward to give. He went to the water's edge prepared to pledge his life, if need be, to the deliverer of his son.

The fish, however, brushed his thanks aside saying, "Do not worry, human; I saved your son with the knowledge that you are poor. The boy himself will reward me later on for, when he reaches manhood he will indeed be rich. All that I ask of you now is that you will remind him from time to time of the fish who saved his life."

Mazwi was delighted to learn from the fish that his son would rise to riches, for he had little to offer the child. So he thanked the good fish once more for his kindness, and returned to his wife; she, of course, was overjoyed not only at the return of her little one, but also at the thought of his wealthy future promised by the fish.

Because he had been returned to them from the very jaws of death, Mphephethwa became even more precious than before in his parents' eyes. His every wish was gratified, his every whim indulged as they assured him of his wealth to come. "Why should I work and toil," he would ask from time to time, "when my ancestors have wealth in store for me?" And before many years had passed he became a lazy good-for-nothing youth who refused to raise a finger to help his hard-working parents.

Matters became worse when his father died, and his mother had many quarrels with her swollen-headed son. When he was eighteen years of age she felt that she could deal with him no longer, so she sent for her brother to come and punish the boy for his waywardness and refusal to listen to her words.

"Come," said the uncle when he had lectured the youth on his duty as a son, "there is work for you to do, for the time has passed that you should live in idleness. Today we will hunt on the mountain top."

The mother prepared some ukhotha* for their journey, and the two set off up the steep mountain. It was a long and strenuous climb but at last, weary and aching in every limb, Mphephethwa reached the summit at his uncle's side. Before them was a huge round boulder, decorated with many figures carved upon it.

The uncle paused to take a strangely plaited bracelet of umsingizane grass from his arm and, mumbling some strange words, took the boy's right hand and drew the bracelet over it. Then, while his uncle muttered some more strange words, the big boulder moved aside, to uncover a gaping hole.

*Roasted stamped green mealies.

"Now, nephew," said the uncle, "the time has come for you to play the part that your ancestors have prepared for you: listen carefully to what I say, for if you miss one single word of my instructions you will most certainly meet your end.

"First and foremost, climb down into this hole. In the cave below you will find three earthen pots placed upside down; now, starting with the first and smallest, you must carefully turn them the right way up. The decision on the course you will follow after this, must rest with you – but should trouble meet you, rub your magic bracelet and any problem will be solved.

"Take all that will be of use to you, then rub the bracelet again and the boulder will return to its place above the hole. May good fortune attend you, my sister's son, for I must now leave you to your own devices." After making sure that Mphephethwa understood his instructions, the uncle turned and left the boy standing on the rim of the big dark hole.

It was a great test for this pampered boy, but he bravely carried out his uncle's orders, descending into the cavern to find the earthen pots exactly as described, placed upside down and half buried in the dust of ages. The one nearest to him was also the smallest, and he lost no time in turning it the right way up.

Imagine his delight when out of it there scrambled many scores of cocks and hens; but his joy was checked as, last of all, there came from the pot a fierce black dog which bared its fangs and made ready to attack him. Fortunately he still held the knobkerrie with which he had left his home – and after a short battle he succeeded in killing the creature.

From the first he passed to the second pot. This one was a great deal larger, and was so firmly embedded in the ground that it took all his strength to move it. However, at last he succeeded and, as he turned it right side up there was a clatter of little hooves, and out scampered flocks of sheep and goats, all bleating with joy at their release.

But this time he had to face an even greater danger than before – for last of all out jumped a great and savage dog which lost no time in attacking and trying to tear him limb from limb. It was a bitter fight that followed, and more than once the big dog nearly pulled him down. But he fought bravely, and finally beat the great brute to the ground, where he killed it.

He sat for a while to regain his breath, then passed on to the third and last pot. It was the largest of them all, and Mphephethwa had to work hard to loosen it from the earth in which it was half buried, and great strength was required to turn it the right way up. But the toil was worth the effort for, from out of it there jumped herds of the finest cattle that Mphephethwa had ever seen. Each herd was in its separate colour – black, white, red and speckled; but last of all there sprang out their guardian, the largest and most savage dog that his wildest imagination could have brought to mind.

This dog too, like those before it, bared its yellow fangs and made ready to attack him, but he knew that however bravely he fought he could not hope to overcome such a fierce and enormous creature. Fortunately, and just in time, he remembered his uncle's last piece of advice and he hastily rubbed the magic bracelet. At once the angry hackles lowered on its back and it advanced to lie down at his feet – where he killed it.

With all three dangers overcome, Mphephethwa looked at his possessions with pride. How, though, could he get them out of their underground prison? he wondered. Again he rubbed the magic talisman, and again he was not disappointed, for the cattle, sheep, goats and fowls all scrambled back into their own pots. These pots he found were now so light that he picked up even the largest of them with ease, and carried them without effort onto the mountain-side.

He rubbed his magic bracelet, and the big round stone rolled back into its old position, blocking up for evermore, the entrance to the cave.

With the big pot balanced safely on his head, and a smaller one beneath each arm, he struggled down the steep and slippery track, taking great care not to drop his precious load. It was a difficult undertaking, but he reached his home without accident, much to his mother's relief, for he had been away for a long time and she feared that ill fortune had befallen him.

Putting down the three pots as he reached his mother's hut, he rubbed his magic bracelet for the last time and, to exclamations of surprise from all the villagers, the fowls and animals poured out of them as before; but this time there were no big dogs to fear! There was dancing and singing far into the night for now the community was rich indeed.

On the following day four of the fattest of the oxen were killed to provide a feast of thanksgiving to Mphephethwa's ancestors for their many gifts and, as the boy's mother dipped her gourd into the river to draw water for the cooking, a big fish raised its head from out of it and addressing her said, "Woman, the time has now come that I should have my reward for restoring your baby son to you eighteen long years ago!"

The woman had almost forgotten the part the fish had played in the prophesy of her son's wealth, but being reminded she asked, "Kind friend, what reward do you wish?"

"My needs are few," replied the fish, "and easily satisfied. All I ask your son to give me is ten each of his newly found possessions."

The mother hastened home to remind Mphephethwa of the fish's kindness in the past, and to tell him of its request. Realising the magnitude of the debt he owed, the boy at once doubled the requirements of the fish and drove them to the river, where the strange creature accepted them with gratitude.

From this time onward the spoilt boy of old became a respected leader of his people. He built a beautiful village and filled it with his many followers. His cattle throve and multiplied – and when the time came for his marriage, his mother chose the most beautiful as well as the most diligent wife in all the land, to share his wealth with him.

And after living for many years to see her grandchildren playing at her hearth, the old mother died and was gathered to her forefathers, content in the knowledge of her son's status and his happiness.

12

KENKEBE AND THE INDAWAS

Kenkebe was a good husband, and there was nothing that he would not do to gratify the wishes of the wife he loved so dearly; in fact he had faced danger many times to satisfy a whim of hers, but she took it all for granted. So he said to her one day, "Wife, I have often risked my life unnecessarily on your account, and I feel that it is time I had some return from you. Therefore please fetch me a drink of water from a spring in which no frogs croak for I am thirsty, and do not like the water with which you have provided me."

This was a task that filled his wife's heart with dismay; where, she wondered, would she find such a spring? All the ones she knew were full of frogs, and it would surely mean a long journey for her into unknown lands. However, she was determined to gratify the wish of the husband who did so much for her so, lifting a water-pot onto her head, she set off to look for a spring that held no frogs.

One by one as she came to them she leaned over and asked, "Are there any frogs in this spring?" and from each in turn came the same reply, "Croak, croak, croak! have you ever seen a spring without a frog in it? Pass on, and tell us when you have found one!"

For three days she continued her fruitless search – until on the fourth day she came to a place where she asked the same question three times; but this time there came no reply. "Then surely there can be no frogs in here!" she exclaimed with joy, as she hurriedly filled her pot with clear, cool water. "I must hasten," she thought, "for surely my good husband will be near to death from thirst!"

When she was about to raise the brimming pot to her head, she saw a feast spread out before her, with many kinds of delicious foods. Not having eaten for so many days, she was as near to exhaustion from lack of food, as her husband surely was from lack of water!

"Whose food is this?" she called out aloud; but there was no reply, nor was there any one in sight to whom to repeat the question so, without more ado she sat down and ate it. But surely what she had eaten was magic food, for the weight of it in her stomach anchored her so firmly to the ground, that she was unable to rise when she had satisfied her hunger.

This was a sorry plight in which to find herself and, as she sat wondering what to do, she was both astonished and frightened to see all kinds of fierce wild animals appearing from the spring. Each as it saw her called out angrily, "So it is YOU who have dared to pollute our Chief's water with your dirty hands, and had the audacity to eat his food?" and each as it passed her gave her a vicious kick, a scratch or a bite.

The poor woman was beside herself with fear and, as she sat trembling, the Great Chief himself, My Lord the Lion, arrived. With a resounding roar that shook the earth he cried, "How DARE you eat my food? For this impertinence you will pay with your life!"

"Spare me, spare me, oh gracious Chief of the Animals!" the unhappy woman sobbed. "I am but a poor woman, sent by her husband to fetch him some water from a spring in which no frogs croak."

The lion, although angry, had mercy upon the woman, and allowed her to take up her pot. So, with a great effort she staggered to her feet and, putting the load upon her head, started her long journey home.

"Husband," she said on arrival, "here is the water for which you crave – but my search was a long one," (she omitted to mention the stolen meal that she had enjoyed at the lion's expense) "and I am in need of food. Please, in payment for the favour that I have done for you, bring me the liver of an Indawa, for nothing else will satisfy the hunger caused by my journey!"

These indawas were strange fierce human-looking creatures that walked on their hands and knees, and lived in the hills several days journey from Kenkebe's home. They were greatly feared, and he fully realised the danger of the undertaking ahead of him.

However, he loved his wife dearly – and had she not just shown *her* love for him, in the dangers of the wilds that she had faced for his sake? So picking up his knobkerrie*, he called his hunting dogs and, with many misgivings in his heart, set out for the country in which these strange creatures lived.

On the third day he reached his destination in a wild and hilly region and, knowing that if they saw him the savage indawas would tear him limb from limb, he decided that his only hope of success lay in pretending

---
*Stick with knob on one end.

to be one of them. He therefore discarded his clothing and, walking on his hands and knees as they did, he approached their settlement.

It was not long before he reached the first collection of little untidy huts. With fear in his heart he crept stealthily towards them – but he found on arrival that, apart from a few small children, the place seemed to be deserted. Gaining courage he went into the clearing to find that there was only one grown-up in sight, and she an old, old woman – obviously too old to take part in the daily search for food. Being poor of sight, she mistook Kenkebe for one of their own kind and welcomed him, offering him some sadly needed food.

Although slightly similar, the indawa language was not easy for him to understand, so he pretended to be dumb and, calming the childrens' fear of his dogs by signs, passed himself off as one of them. But there was one little indawa boy who was very much sharper than the others. "Grandmother," he kept saying, "what kind of an indawa is this? See, his skin is smooth, and his feet and hands are *very* clean!"

"Be quiet, my grandchild," the old woman rebuked him each time, slapping and pinching him as she sent him out of the hut to play. Not satisfied, however, the boy came back time and again, each time with another question about their strange guest; but each time the grandmother sent him away with slaps and pinches.

In the evening the rest of the indawa family returned weary from a fruitless day of hunting and, throwing themselves upon their grass beds took small notice of the stranger in their midst – nor of the small boy's suspicion of him.

When morning came Kenkebe arose with the others and, whistling to his dogs, set out on the daily hunt with his host and family. At first the dogs caused great consternation among his fellow hunters, but soon the indawas began to marvel at their prowess, cheering and praising them and their clever owner as they ran down one buck after another.

This was just as well for Kenkebe, for the unaccustomed mode of walking on his hands and knees caused him great pain and, without their interest in his dogs, the indawas would soon have noticed his deception. Instead, he was looked upon as a hero as they carried home a large supply of meat that night and, trying to hide the agony he suffered from raw and swollen knees, he soon sank gratefully down to rest.

When morning came, his knees were so sore and stiff that the indawas signalled him to remain at home, while they went to hunt as usual. "Now," thought Kenkebe when the hunting party was well on its way up the mountain, "is my chance to carry out this sorry task of mine," so he killed the old grandmother indawa and, hastily removing her liver, set off with all the speed his aching knees would permit, on his long journey home.

The terrified children set up such a screaming and yelling that the indawas soon heard them, and came hurrying home. On the way they met the suspicious little indawa boy who was running to tell them what had happened. "Now, tell me, was I right, or was I wrong?" he asked them. "I told you that he was not one of us, but all I got was beatings. I want you to make my grandmother alive again!"

The angry indawas lost no time in following in Kenkebe's tracks, and although fear lent him wings as he fled for his very life, his painful knees slowed his pace and when only a short distance from his home, they caught up with him.

It was then that Kenkebe's dogs showed their devotion to their master, for they set upon the indawas with such ferocity that his pursuers were not only defeated but were killed, and Kenkebe was able to present his wife with many livers, instead of only one!

In the end it turned out that the two dangerous tasks that the husband and wife had set each other, were a blessing to them both, for each now realised the foolishness of trying to prove the other's love, when in doing so each had nearly lost the other. Therefore, they humbly asked forgiveness one from the other, and lived happily and trustingly together to the end of their days.

13

THE MAGIC WATER-POT

Mzanywa was the proud owner of a magic earthen water-pot, or ingcazi, and so precious was this possession that he would allow no one to handle it but himself. And who could blame him, for did it not turn the sparkling water from the spring into mellow beer, or to sweetest milk at his wish? Surely a pot with magical properties such as these, was safe in no other hands than his?

However, Vuyile, his first-born, longed more and more as she grew in years, to carry water in this magic pot. "Surely," she thought, "some of its magic will be transferred to me if only I could carry water in it once!"

Her chance came one day when her father and her mother Mamasomi went to a dance at a neighbouring village. "Daughter, fetch some water for me to cook the evening meal when I return," her mother called over her shoulder as she left, "and care for Hluphekile while we are gone." Hluphekile was Vuyile's younger sister; a jealous and naughty little girl of six years old.

"Now," said Vuyile to herself when her parents were out of sight, "at last here is an opportunity for me to carry out my wish – for who is there to stop me? None need ever know, and I shall soon discover what magic properties my father's wonderful ingcazi holds for me!" And placing the precious pot upon her head she walked towards the river with Hluphekile hurrying along the path behind her, trying to keep up with her sister's long strides. But Hluphekile was a fat little girl, and her legs were very short, so she was soon left farther and farther behind.

"So! she would forget me?" the child muttered angrily to herself as she lost sight of her big sister. "I will teach her not to ignore me as she does!" and she gathered a small handful of the grass that grew along the edge of the path, and tied it to an equal sized bunch from the other side of the path, forming a good strong knot.

She chuckled to herself as she thought of the probable consequences of the trick that so many generations of children before her had played on elder sisters. But one trap was not enough; sometimes the stride of the foot passed *over* a single trap – she must make some more.

She ran a short way farther along the path after her sister, then tied two more bunches of grass across the path – and farther on yet another two. She hugged her small shoulders with delight as she sat down at the side of the path to watch the result of her mischief.

She did not have long to wait before Vuyile, her eyes straight in front of her (the easier to balance the precious water-pot upon her head) came striding back along the path. Catching her toe in the first trap to meet her, she stumbled, but with great presence of mind recovered herself and grasped the pot in time to save it from crashing to the ground.

"Ech!" she exclaimed, not seeing Hluphekile hiding behind some bushes. "A thousand plagues on those naughty herd boys; wait until I discover who has tricked me in this manner!" and with a good-natured laugh she continued on her way.

With the grass brushing her knees and almost hiding the pathway as she hurried on, it was impossible for her to see Hluphekile's second trap, and once more she caught her foot. This time she landed on her knees, and by some miracle she saved the pot again.

She looked around her in anger this time for the little herd-boys whom she still blamed for the trick. Seeing no one, she decided to hurry home to leave the water there before returning to punish the naughty little rascals.

After a short rest she continued on her homeward journey, carefully watching the path for further pranks. But the last trap was too well concealed for her to see, and the heavy pot upon her head made it difficult for her to examine the path too closely so, catching her foot in it, she fell down. This time there was a sickening crash, and her father's precious magic ingcazi lay shattered in a dozen fragments on the ground. "Oh!" she cried, horrified at what she saw, "my father's *magic pot!* Whatever shall I do?"

Too frightened of her father's anger to return home, she sat weeping at the side of the pathway. Soon Hluphekile caught up with her and, laughing at the broken pot said, "Our father will thrash you when he knows what you have done!" and she went on her way alone.

In the evening when her parents returned to their hut they found Hluphekile there alone, so asked where her elder sister was? "Oh," answered Hluphekile, "she broke her father's magic pot, and is afraid to return to her home!"

"What is a pot, although it is a magic one," said Mzanywa, "against

my flesh and blood? Go, Hluphekile, and fetch your sister home. The hut is lonely without her happiness and laughter."

Out into the night the younger sister went, and soon found Vuyile cold and weeping under the shelter of some bushes by the path. But Hluphekile had not come to the end of her mischief yet for, besides being a naughty little girl, she was very jealous of her elder sister's easy laughing good nature, and of her parents' imagined greater love for the elder one; therefore she decided to follow up her mischief with deceit, so she said, "I come from our father with this message from him; 'Go, never again do I wish to set eyes on the breaker of my magic pot!'"

With all hope for forgiveness gone, Vuyile wandered cold and miserable into the night, while Hluphekile returned to her home to tell her parents that she had searched for her sister in vain.

All through the night Vuyile tramped the countryside, until she was completely lost. Day after day she searched for some human habitation without success. She lived on the fruits and roots that she found growing by the wayside and was in a sorry state when she saw a light that twinkled in the distance. Hastily she made for its companionship, hoping to find food and shelter at last.

When she reached the hut from which it came, she found several people sitting round a brightly lighted fire. As she stood timidly at the open door a voice from inside said, "Night is no time for one as young and beautiful as you, to be wandering abroad; child, from where do you come, and why are you alone?"

Sadly Vuyile told the tale of the broken ingcazi and of how, having been turned from her home by her father, she had wandered in the wilds until completely lost. "Come in," said the good-looking owner of the voice as he came to the doorway. "All this land belongs to me, and I bid you welcome to my kraal."

On the following morning he sent for her and said, "My child, you are homeless and disowned. For a long time now I have searched for someone who can turn this heap of rubble into much needed iron. My warriors are sadly short of spears, and my blacksmiths' anvils have been forced to silence for lack of it. Do this for me, and I will make you my foremost wife," and he pointed to a large mound of rubble beside him.

"Ah!" she thought, "perhaps the magic of my father's pot has transferred itself to me!" and picking up the two grinding stones nearby as the chief turned away, she took a piece of the rubble and hopefully started to crush it. But try as she would, no iron appeared – and she was just about to bury her face in her hands to stifle her sobs of disappointment, when a little tikoloshe or gnome, passed by. Arrested by her sobs he came up to her and putting his skinny hand upon her shoulder said, "Little one, why are you sad?"

"I am homeless," she sobbed, "and unless by magic I can turn this rubble into iron for the chief who rules this land, can find no shelter for my head." She then told the tikoloshe of all that had befallen her, and of the chief's promise to make her the leading lady in the land if she could carry out his wish.

The tikoloshe was a scheming little creature, as are most of his kind. "Now this," he thought, "is my chance to obtain a well-born human child to bring up as my slave. When he has learned my tricks, I will use him for my magic works!" So he whispered in her ear, "should I do your task for you, what will you give me in return?"

To become the wife of such a handsome and powerful chief was indeed a temptation to the homeless girl, so she replied without hesitation, "I will give you what you ask."

Without another word the tikoloshe took the grinding stones from her and bent to his task. For a while he worked in silence, stopping from time to time to throw the iron to swell the pile in front of him. "My reward," he said at length, "will be your first-born son; there," he continued, tossing the last of the iron to join the rest, "your son is bound to me. When he has passed his second year, I will come and beckon from the doorway of your hut, and you must fulfil your pledge," and he continued on his way.

Her heart thumped wildly with excitement, but demurely she sat and waited – for the custom of the land forbade her to hasten to her lord as it was her wish to do, to claim the reward that she had won. Instead, she waited humbly on his pleasure.

Before long he came, and unbelievingly he stood as though rooted to the ground. "Child!" he cried excitedly, "do my eyes play me false?" He bent down and ran his hands over the pile before he would believe it was real.

There was merrymaking and feasting when the marriage took place, and cattle were sent to Vuyile's father who came over the hills to bless her. In the course of time as the foremost lady in the land the bride settled down happily in her new home, and when a little son was born to her she had no thought except for the joys of motherhood.

However, as the first year, and then the second one crept past, an icy fear laid its fingers on her heart as she remembered her promise to the little tikoloshe. But the little gnome had not forgotten; and one day called his people to him and said, "Today I shall go to claim my human child – but all may not go well with me. The magic of her father's broken ingcazi still surrounds his mother, and its powers may be too strong for me. Watch my hut; should it burst into flames while I am gone, then mourn me as dead." And after he had said these words, he set off towards Vuyile's home.

He found the girl sitting in her hut with the baby on her lap. A strange feeling of magnetism made her turn her head towards the open door. There, leaning insolently against the timbers stood the tikoloshe, and he raised his hand and beckoned to her. At first she turned her back to him, refusing to acknowledge him or to recognise his beckoning hand; so he went inside the hut and, grasping her by the shoulder with his skinny fingers, turned her to him and pointed to the lovely child upon her lap.

"Ah!" she cried, "you *cannot* take him from me. Cut out my heart instead, but leave my child to me!"

"What!" screamed the tikoloshe, "would you *bargain* with me?" and he tried to snatch the baby from Vuyile. But she was both tall and strong, so she held the little one above her head, where the little gnome could not reach him. Angrier and angrier grew the tikoloshe as he was thwarted until, in exasperation he began to choke.

Suddenly he shrieked, and Vuyile saw a jagged piece of pottery hurtling through the air towards him. Straight for the little creature's head it flew and, hitting him on the temple, he fell groaning to the ground.

Vuyile watched fascinated, as he lay twitching at her feet, but soon all movement ceased, and she knew that he was dead. She picked his body up to hide it from her husband, so that he would never know her secret and, as she did so, she saw lying where he had fallen, a piece of broken ingcazi with a familiar pattern on it – and she realised that her father's magic pot had made amends for all the trouble it had brought to her . . . while at his home his people watched the tikoloshe's hut burst into flames, and they knew that they would see him no more.

14

SITHEMBILE AND HER SNAKE

In Xhosaland long ago, when witches and wizards cast their evil spells on those who in any way displeased them, there lived a wealthy chief with his three wives.

The eldest and most important wife was childless, and this annoyed her very much indeed for, according to Xhosa law and custom her son (should she have one) would rule the tribe when the chief, her husband, died. Being childless, the status that should by right be hers, was threatened – and she brooded incessantly on the matter, and all the while her cruel heartless nature caused the villagers to lose sympathy for her in her disappointment, so that they grew to hate her more and more instead.

The woman was not only cruel; she was well known for her powers of witchery. This made her feared as well as hated. No one dared to thwart her for in her hut, (into which none but herself might enter) were a magic stick and two gourds. In these gourds were powerful potions, and woe betide the person at whom she pointed this magic stick after she had doctored it with the potions, for immediately the luckless one would be changed into whatever creature she cared to name!

The second wife had a baby son who was as lovable as he was handsome – a favourite far and near, and his name was Nyezi. He would be the ruler one day and was therefore doubly precious in the eyes of all; in the eyes of everyone, that is, except in those of the wicked sorceress who, from the day that he was born, had planned to do away with him when a suitable opportunity arrived.

This leaves the third wife – Nomvula; she was as gentle and kind as was the mother of little Nyezi, and her three pretty daughters played happily with their half-brother all day long.

In making her plans to destroy the little heir, the foremost wife had to keep her wits about her, for her wicked deeds were known throughout the land – and she knew that if any harm befell the boy, the blame would at once be laid on her. Slowly and carefully therefore, she set about to work her wickedness upon the child and, observing this Nomvula approached his mother saying, "Sister, as our husband's foremost wife hates us and is jealous of our children, I feel that it would be safer for you to share my hut with me; then we can together watch over our little ones, and also benefit by the warnings of the magic horn my mother gave to me."

Nyezi's mother gladly agreed to this kindness, and the two younger wives felt secure in each other's company. The wicked wife was also pleased at the arrangement "For," she thought to herself, "with these two foolish women together, I can work my will on both of them at once!" and she patiently bided her time.

Little Nyezi was then three years old, and growing in importance as he was growing in charm, while among those who loved him most of all was a little girl who lived in a neighbouring village. She often came to play with him and his three little half-sisters; her name was Sithembile.

"Surely our little ones are safe by day, in view of all our friends," thought the mothers as the three children played happily in the sunshine. But when evening came, they were kept indoors so that no harm could possibly come to them during the hours of darkness.

"Ah!" chuckled the foremost wife, "they think that they are safe! but let them wait until the hour of midnight, for then my magic is most potent, and the mothers will be sleeping."

Night after night she crept round the village listening at the doors, to make certain that everyone slept. One night she felt that she was safe so, taking the ointment from one of the magic gourds she smeared it on her stick; next she took the gourd with liquid in it and stole quietly to the hut where the mothers and four children slept.

Nearer she crept, and nearer! Again she chuckled as she thought with what ease she would turn that foolish child into just whatever beast she chose! She was about to push aside the little rush door when, to her great annoyance she heard the two women laughing and talking . . . while inside the hut Nomvula's magic horn stood up as it sensed danger in the air and sang softly,

"Nomvula, Nomvula, my grandmother's child!
 Some evil is coming to you,
Nomvula, my grandmother's child.
 Here comes your sister-in-law,

> Nomvula, my grandmother's child!
> She wants your children –
> Nomvula, my grandmother's child –
> Because she has none of her own,
> Nomvula, my grandmother's child!"

Time and again the same thing happened as the sorceress made further attempts to find the mothers off their guard – but each time the magic horn warned them of the approaching danger, and each time the two women inside the hut stoked up the fire and laughed and chatted to let the wicked woman on the other side of the door know that they were aware of her presence. Each time, too, the foremost wife shook her fists in anger as she turned away frustrated, to ask herself if those stupid women never slept?

Once the danger had passed the magic horn lay down again, and the mothers knew that they and their children were safe for another night. Over and over again the magic horn saved them all in this manner, and during this time little Nyezi grew more beautiful as he left his babyhood behind him.

In the end, the foremost wife became so infuriated at the constant night-time vigil of the two mothers, that in desperation she struck one day in broad daylight while Nyezi and the three little girls were playing near their mothers' hut. Deliberately she took her magic stick and, smearing it well with the ointment from the gourd, ran to where the children played.

First she splashed the three half-sisters with the liquid, and immediately they fell unconcious to the ground. After this she pointed the deadly stick at little Nyezi as, her eyes blazing with hatred she chanted, "Now, child of my husband, at last I am able to work my will on you! In future your mother will have no son with whom to taunt me. Instead she will have a SNAKE!" and as the last word left her lips, the boy changed into a long and ugly snake.

It happened that Sithembile was coming through the village to join her friends at play when this dreadful happening took place. Her screams quickly brought the men and women to the scene, and they were in time to see the three little girls still lying where they had fallen, while a big black snake twined itself about them.

"Who," asked the horrified people, "could have done this wicked thing? And where is the witch who has done it?" Everybody looked at once towards the sorceress' hut – but there she sat, complacently smoking her long wooden pipe as much as to say, "Yes, hated child, I have got you at last; but no one can prove my guilt!"

The three little girls soon recovered from their faint, and were very surprised to find the villagers gazing anxiously at them, and to hear a big black snake address the people saying, "Do not weep, my friends – the time will come when the one who has cast this spell upon me will regret her deed. I will come back some day to rule you, though, because snakes and humans cannot mix, I will in future live in the river where my kind belong – and there I will grow to maturity. When the time is ripe, one who loves me will break the evil spell that binds me to this reptile shape, and will bring me back to you." After saying these words he slithered through the village and disappeared from sight.

Nyezi's father, heart-broken at the loss of his only son, tried to comfort his weeping wife. Realising that his jealous foremost wife had caused this mischief, he drove her from his home. This, however, did not suit the wicked woman's plans for by now she had decided to destroy not only Nyezi's mother, but her own husband too. Therefore she repeatedly tried to return to her old home, giving her husband the excuse that she was lonely without him.

The chief, however, knowing her as he did, saw through her guile, so on the next occasion when she came, he pretended to welcome her and even invited her to share the comfort of his hut; and being tired after her long journey, the woman slept soundly.

This was exactly what the husband had planned so, quietly smearing the magic ointment on her magic stick, he held it behind him as he woke her up. "Now, wife," he said, "you must listen to what I have to say. All your wicked deeds have been done against my will and against my people, and you have not maintained a single custom of this home – hiding always behind my people's fear of your magic stick. My only son has been lost to me by your sorcery and wickedness, and now you come back hatching something worse! Be ready, woman, for the death you have prepared for me!"

He pointed the magic stick straight at the wicked creature's heart, and she fell dead upon the bed from which he had roused her.

There was jubilation throughout the village when news spread through it that they need no longer fear either the woman or her sorcery, and the chief's subjects were delighted when they learned that her own magic had killed her.

*

The time has come, however, to go back to little Sithembile. As her father had no son to herd his many cows for him, it fell to the lot of his only daughter to do the task – therefore day in, day out, year in, year out Sithembile drove his herd to the pastures across the river in which Nyezi lived out his life as a big black snake.

With equal regularity Nyezi waited at the ford to watch the girl drive her father's cattle through, and to have a word with her. At first she shrank from contact with his reptile form, and although she longed to comfort him in his loneliness, she kept him at a distance.

Notwithstanding this, as the years passed, so did the snake's love for his childhood sweetheart grow until, when they were both eighteen years of age Nyezi said to her one evening as she drove the cattle home, "Sithembile, the time has come at last for me to regain my human form – but this can only be done through one who loves me. Listen carefully to what I say, then follow my directions with the greatest care.

"When you close your father's cattle in tonight, look around to make sure that no one watches you; then take an earthen pot and fill it with dung from the cattle in the byre. Go with this to the byre where my father keeps his herd and you will see, among the many cattle there, a big white ox without a spot or blemish. Take him gently by the horns, and lead him straight to me."

Although Sithembile was afraid, she carefully carried out the snake's instructions and, before the moon had risen was on her way back to the river, leading by his horns the big white ox.

She reached her journey's end and, as the huge snake slithered up the bank to meet her, her heart thumped wildly with fear; but she mastered her feelings as he said to her, "Take some of the cowdung from the earthen pot, Sithembile, and smear it on my body."

Her courage almost failed as she did the reptile's bidding, and she was relieved when, as she completed her task, he turned and disappeared beneath the water. Her heart thumped more wildly than ever when she saw him rise again – but this time it thumped with wonder and with joy, for the scaly reptile head had disappeared, and in its place was the handsome head of the little boy Nyezi, though grown older.

The reptile body now came close to her, stretching its great coils along the river bank, and Nyezi's head said to her, "Sithembile, smear more cowdung on me as you did before." After she had done his bidding for a second time, he once more disappeared beneath the surface of the water.

She watched the spot at which he sank with growing fascination and excitement as first the human head, and then a pair of hands came into view – and the reptile tail lashed the surface as he swam quickly to her side. "Once more, Sithembile; once more! and this time smear me *well*," he said. "When this is done, drive my father's ox into the water after me."

Lightheartedly now, Sithembile smeared him, caring little for the feel of his reptile skin – and using *all* the dung remaining in the earthen pot. And the white ox followed willingly as Nyezi plunged for the third time into the water.

It seemed a long, long while to the waiting girl before she saw the water part again. This time she held her breath in wonder, for there came out of the depths a youth of wondrous beauty, mounted on the snow-white flawless ox, and he hailed her joyfully as he reached her side. "Eh! Sithembile, it is good to feel my arms and legs again . . . but there is still **ONE MORE THING FOR YOU TO DO**! Take the ox by his horns, and lead us to my father's home."

This the girl did happily; and as the village came in sight, the ox lifted his head and bellowed so loudly that the villagers rushed from their huts to find out the reason for all the noise.

The sight that met their eyes was a beautiful one indeed, for the full moon shone on the happy girl as she led her childhood sweetheart astride his snow-white mount, back to his father's home. A great shout of joy arose from every throat as the people realised that Sithembile had released their chief's long-lost son from the spell that had bound him for so many years, to the body of a cold-blooded snake.

On the following day his father and mother prepared a magnificent feast of thanksgiving to welcome their son back to his home; and to add to his pleasure, his three half-sisters, now plump and lovely maidens, came from their mother's home to join in the merrymaking and fun.

But the story does not end here for, a few months later there was a much more wonderful celebration, to mark the marriage between Nyezi and Sithembile. The whole countryside rejoiced, and in the fullness of time, when the old chief was gathered to his ancestors, Nyezi ruled in his stead. He was greatly blessed in the devotion and companionship of his beloved Sithembile, and ruled wisely and well until the end of his days.

PRONUNCIATION GUIDE AND GLOSSARY

Novile	No-vi-le.	
zim	zim	cannibal.
Nomathanga	No-ma-tha-nga	little pumpkin.
phuma	phu-ma	come forth.
hlala	hla-la	stay here.
Mavile	Ma-vi-le.	
Mpunzikazi	Mpu-nzi-kazi.	
Mpunzanyane	Mpu-nza-nya-ne.	
mabele	ma-be-le	one of the surghums.
Nomehlomancinane	No-me-hlo-ma-nci-na-ne	of the small eyes.
Nomahamle	No-ma-ham-le.	
umphako	um-pha-ko	food for the road.
Integu	In-teg-u.	
Mdinini	Mdi-ni-ni.	
Nyengula	Nye-ngu-la.	
amasi	a-ma-si	curdled milk.
umphothulo	um-pho-thu-lo	stamped roast mealies.
Nondwe	No-ndw-e.	
Deliwe	De-li-we.	
Mbebe	Mbe-be.	
Nomdudo	No-mdu-do.	
Velaphi	Ve-la-phi.	
imvaba	im-va-ba	skin sack in which milk is curdled.
ntsika	in-tsi-ka	centre pole that holds up the roof.
Malumi	Ma-lu-mi.	
Ant-bear		wild animal that eats ants, lives in underground warrens.
Monitor		large lizard.
Mbulumakhasane	Mbulu-ma-kha-sa-ne.	
khokhothi	kho-kho-thi	little slave.
Thangalimlibo	Tha-nga-lim-libo	the stem of the pumpkin.
Lungelo	Lu-nge-lo.	
isikonde	i-si-ko-nde	wild carrots.
Dantalasele	Danta-la-se-le.	

Mphephethwa	....	....	M-phe-phe-thwa.
Nomvula	....	....	Nom-vula.
Sithembile	....	....	Si-the-mbi-le.
Ingcazi	....	....	Ing-caz-i .... earthen pot for carrying water.
Vuyile	....	....	Vu-yi-le.
Mamasomi	....	....	Mam-a-somi.
Hluphekile	....	....	Hlu-phe-ki-le.
tikoloshe	....	....	ti-ko-lo-she .... small supernatural gnomelike creature.
Kenkebe	....	....	Ke-nke-be.
Indawa	....	....	I-nda-wa.

MATABELE

Illustrated by
SYLVIA BAXTER

FOREWORD

The folklore of a People is very much part of its life – a most revealing part. To know something of it is a royal road to understanding. Some of the stories in this book will seem vaguely familiar to those who have read *Uncle Remus*. But that is not due to plagiarism or to coincidence, but simply to the fact that both are part of the thought of a great continent we are just beginning to understand.

Perhaps I am biassed, for I was one of the children who grew up surrounded by the atmosphere of these stories, but they seem to me to have a kinder, and for that matter more attractive, twist than those stories taken to America by the West African slaves. Whether this is right or not, the small people of Zimbabwe, and elsewhere, will find them vastly entertaining and full of knowledge of nature as she manifests herself in our own country.

R. C. Tredgold

THE RIGHT HONOURABLE SIR ROBERT CLARKSON TREDGOLD, K.C.M.G.

INTRODUCTION

It was a strange new life for a little five-year-old girl like me to go to. No parties, not many schools, hardly *any* children; and certainly no circuses or movies, or even ice-creams, in the Zimbabwe of over fifty years ago.

But there was something that was better than all these things put together. There was the great big wild Zimbabwean Bush, and there was the nicest little boy in the world, who took me under his wing soon after Mother and I arrived from Johannesburg to join my Father and two nearly grown up brothers, Lee and Tommy, on our new Zimbabwean farm.

After a long train journey, our engine chugged its way into the tiny station of Hartley with its few tin buildings, at 2 o'clock on a pitch black morning.

We strained our eyes into the darkness, and saw my father swinging a lantern, with Tommy, the younger of my two brothers, standing by his side.

They led us through the little white station gate, to the farm wagon, that was to take us to Lambourne, our new home . . . Inspanned to it were sixteen long-horned oxen, while holding the leading thong was a small and very sleepy African boy of about eight years old, crouching over a flickering camp fire.

He gazed with interest at the small white girl; possibly one of the first he had ever seen. He stretched his little naked body in the flickering firelight and rubbed out the flames with his hard little foot, as he pulled the big oxen round to join the driver, who came out of the shadows with a long whip over his shoulder, and we jolted back to the station shed to load up our heavy luggage.

At last we set out for the farm. There were two deck chairs on the floor of the wagon for my mother and father, while Tommy and I sat on the luggage. The driver, with an occasional crack from his enormous whip, trudged in the shadows beside the oxen.

The little African boy acted as leader to the oxen, pulling on the thong that was tied around their enormous horns, and they followed him through thick and thin.

The road was very wet after a heavy storm a few hours earlier and it was not long before we heard the sound of racing water. Just then the little leader and the first two oxen commenced to cross what had been, earlier in the evening, a small stream.

By the light of the lantern we saw him almost swept away, as he struggled through the tearing water. The two leading oxen went in fearlessly after him, and the other fourteen followed. But the force of the water was so great that the little boy, oxen, wagon and all of us were nearly washed down the river. The strength of the big beasts saved us all.

It was not long after our arrival that I came to know the only other settler's child in our district. His name was Farewell, and as all our thoughts and our interests were the same, we spent nearly all our days together. We bird-nested, we hunted, and we played together. We haunted the wagon, accompanying it on most of its farm work, and we pestered its good-natured driver, Chakuti, for stories of the birds and animals around us.

This paradise could not last for ever, and in time we were sent to Boarding School. But there were always the holidays to which to look forward, and we ticked off the days of learning one by one. Once back on the farm, our joys commenced anew; camping, Chakuti's stories, bird-nesting, hunting, and all the other fun.

The little tales that follow were spread over our childhood years, and belong to our Zimbabwe of long ago.

1

THE HARE'S ROPE TRICK

One day Farewell and I went out with Chakuti and the wagon to collect a load of tall thatching grass, for re-thatching the workers' huts, to make them waterproof before the big rains came.

It was during the month of October, which was always a time of excitement for, apart from the great nesting activities among the birds, young of all the wild animals were being born. We never knew what strange little pets would find their ways into our hands at this time.

No African could resist the young of anything he found. Even tiny featherless birds were welcome in their stew pots, and our hearts bled for the little creatures. Whenever we could we would rescue them, by bribe or by threat, and with great patience and love, we would rear them when possible.

On this particular occasion we were trying to trap a big leguaan (water monitor) on the banks of the Umfuli River, while the two men and Chakuti cut and loaded the long grass.

Suddenly there was a shout from one of them, which was taken up by the other two, and with sticks raised high above their heads, they raced in our direction.

Fleeing in front of them, and making straight for where we stood, was the tiniest little hare that I had ever seen.

He was almost too terrified to run, and zig-zagged into a bush at our side, where he tried to make himself look as much like a dead leaf as possible. But it is indeed a clever creature that can hide from the sharp eyes of an African, and with whoops of joy, they pounced upon him.

"No!" I cried, "do not kill Vundhla; my money-box has money in it – for has not my birthday just passed? What meat can you make of so small a creature? Give him to me; I shall give you money when we get home."

So the terrified little creature was put into my hands, and we tried to comfort him.

Gradually we won his confidence and, drop by drop, we put a mixture of milk, sugar and water, into his tiny mouth.

We made him a big hutch and put the tiniest collar on his little neck. Daily we took him for walks among the ploughed fields on the end of a very long string. There he chose his own dainties for supper, and romped and played.

Week by week he grew, and was a long, lanky half-grown hare, when one day I had just tied the string to his collar and was taking him out of his hutch, when some visitors arrived. I popped him back again, string and all, with a promise to take him out later.

No sooner had our guests departed, than we took him to the lands for his promised run, and he straight away commenced to frisk and play. As soon as the string grew taut, he gave a tiny tug; there was a sudden slackening at my end of the string, and with a kick-up of his two hind legs, my pet ran free.

I ran after him, but Vundhla had not bitten the string almost through for nothing. He lost no time in returning to the freedom from whence he had come.

Chakuti was driving the wagon across the field with a load of kraal manure for ploughing into the land for the coming crops, at the time, and saw the sad end to my 'tug of war'. "Ei, Nkosizana,"* he called out, "how do you think you can win, pulling a 'tug o' war' against the cunning Vundhla, when even the great Mvuu and Chipembere cannot pull him over the hill?"

The idea was so ridiculous that I dried my tears and said, "But Chakuti, that could never be! There is no strength in a hare."

"Not strength, perhaps, but great cunning!" he said mysteriously.

We climbed up on to the wagon as it bumped over the mealie stubble, and begged to be told about Vundla, Mvuu and Chipembere. I think that

---

*Young mistress.

Chakuti was sorry for us in the loss of our pet, for he commenced straight away.

It was when I worked as a child, near the great Zambesi River, that I first heard of the cunning of Vundhla.

Always he has been one for playing jokes, as you know, and none of the creatures of the wilds trust him, though time and again they still fall victim to his sweet tongue.

It happened that one day he came across a great hippopotamus bull, grazing peacefully on the bank of the big river.

"Good morning Uncle," said Vundhla in his kindest tones, "you look fine and powerful this morning."

Mvuu was well aware of his ugliness but he prided himself on his strong limbs. Great was his pleasure when people remarked on his strength.

"Yes," answered Mvuu, "it is well known among all, that I am the strongest of all the animals. None can pit his strength against mine!"

"Yet, Uncle," boasted Vundhla, "for all my smallness, and the thinness of my legs, I can beat you in a tug o' war!"

"Go away, yours is silly talk," answered Mvuu, "whoever heard of a ridiculous little thing like *you*, beating one of the race of Mvuu in pulling?"

"There is a very special medicine for strength, given to me by Mpisi the Witch Doctor. Well must you know of the strength of *his* medicines."

Vundhla was in a wicked mood, and the more the hippo laughed at such foolishness, the more did Vundhla beg Mvuu to test his strength. In the end Mvuu agreed, for the sake of peace and quiet, to pull the tug o' war.

Vundhla went off dancing with joy, to plait a long, strong rope from a creeping grass that grew on a bank nearby, telling Mvuu to wait until his return.

When he had made his rope, he tied it with care to one of Mvuu's legs, saying as he carried the other end over a little rise nearby, "When I say PULL, you must *really* pull – for I am going to beat you!"

Having carried the other end of the rope over the rise, he crept up to Chipembere the rhinoceros, who he knew was sleeping not far away. He also carried a handful of fierce little red ants, well wrapped up in a leaf – and these he carefully put one by one into the ear of the sleeping rhinoceros.

After a few minutes Chipembere sat up with a jerk, and began a great shaking of his head, and scratching of his ear.

When Vundhla could stop his laughter, he went up to him and said in his sweetest voice. "Good day, Uncle; I was just coming to warn you that you are sleeping near the home of the little Red Devils. I see one now, coming out of your ear! Let me remove it for you," and with a great show of care, he pushed the remaining ants further into the rhino's ear.

"That was good of you," said Chipembere; "Your paw is of a size that can fit with comfort into my ear, whereas my own big foot has difficulty in dealing with such small matters."

"Maybe my feet *are* small, Uncle, but I am *very* strong. Let me tie this piece of rope around your leg, and I will pull you right over that little rise!"

Chipembere laughed for a long time at Vundhla's boasting, moving as he did so, across to another grassy bed, away from the supposed ants' nest.

But Vundhla followed him, dragging his long rope after him. "Come on, Uncle, I am feeling as strong as ten oxen today. PLEASE have a tug o' war with me!"

"Oh, alright," said the rhino good naturedly. After all, Vundhla *had* helped him in the matter of the ants; so he stretched out one of his hind legs, and Vundhla lost no time in tying his rope round it.

"Now," said Vundhla, "when I get to the top of that little rise, I will shout PULL – and when I say pull, I MEAN pull – or I will pull *you* right into the Zambesi river!"

Chipembere laughed aloud at the hare's boasting, and settled down for another doze, though as the ants worked deeper and deeper into his ear, a new scratching began.

Meanwhile Vundhla took himself off to the top of the rise, where he hid in the grass before he shouted "PULL!"

As the words left his mouth, all the ants began to bite at the same time, and with a roar of rage the rhino bolted, dragging Mvuu, who was quietly sleeping at the other end of the rope, half way up the rise; and then a great pulling began.

Vundhla laughed so loudly that Mvuu and Chipembere stopped their tug of war, and turned to see where the noise came from. There at the top of the rise was Vundhla, holding his sides with mirth, and each knew that he had been tricked!

With lowered head, and rage in his heart, each from his own side charged up the rise, hoping to trample the wicked hare to death, so that no one would ever know what a fool he had made of them.

Vundhla, however, was too quick for them. He jumped to the side as their heads met over the rise, and the crash of their collision was like a loud clap of thunder.

In a tremendous rage now, each against the other, a bitter fight commenced between Mvuu and Chipembere. To this day, still do the wild folk talk of it.

After a time, though, they caught sight of Vundhla, rolling on the ground with laughter and this reminded them of the cause of their trouble. They thereupon once more charged Vundhla – but you know the speed of the hare! The more they chased, the more he laughed at and dodged them, telling all whom he saw, of the foolishness of their quarrel.

And to this day does Chipembere think that the fierce little red ants are still in his ears – some say that they went even further, and now live in his brain – and it is this that makes him so uncertain in his temper.

And Mvuu? He searches up and down the river banks, hoping that one day he will catch Vundhla, and throw him to the ever waiting crocodiles!

*

"So you see, Nkosizana, Vundhla is wise in the ways of ropes!"

2

WHICH TELLS OF HOW THE HIPPOPOTAMUS LEFT THE FOREST LANDS, AND BECAME A CREATURE OF THE RIVERS AND LAKES

On the last day of one of Farewell's visits to Lambourne, Lee let us borrow Chakuti for a day of birds-nesting, and after a great deal of discussion we decided to follow the Umfuli River (which bordered our farm) as far up as the Hippo Pool. Who could say that we might not even catch a glimpse of the shy creatures that had given their name to that deep and fascinating pool!

Farewell lost no time in collecting the precious saloon rifle, and a goodly supply of ammunition, while I raced to Mother for something for our lunch. There were cold sweet-potatoes in the safe, and I hastily buttered some thick slices of bread. Meat we would have scorned to take. This we would shoot for ourselves, to grill on the glowing embers of our midday fire.

I, as usual, was entrusted with the boxes for the birds' eggs. Chakuti stuck a small axe into his belt, and completed his load by slinging the bag with the food in it, over his shoulder. Farewell carried the most important things of all, i.e., the gun and the ammunition, and in no time we were swinging, in single file, down the path to the river.

It was a day of glorious sunshine, and the joy of Spring was in the air. All the forest trees were festooned with blossoms, and the air was heavy with their scent.

The little grey squirrels raced, from time to time, across the short green grass from one tree to another, while the big blue-throated lizards gazed impudently at us from the tree trunks.

The gay cicada almost dazed us with the piercing shrillness of his voice, while from time to time a Pennant-wing Nightjar would rise with startling suddenness from almost beneath our feet, and flit like a shadow, to become invisible once more among the undergrowth a few metres away.

Their eggs were practically the colour of the bare earth on which they were laid, and it took a sharp eye to find them.

It took a sharp eye also, to spot the mother birds, flitting furtively from their tree nests; but many a rare egg was added to our collection that day.

Our search absorbed our interest to such an extent, that the sun was right overhead before we came in sight of the Hippo Pool.

"Ssh! If *only* we could see Mvuu," sighed Farewell.

"Wait," hissed Chakuti, "*Mvuu*, did you not hear that noise? Like a sigh, as he went down? THAT is why he is called MVUU. The sun rose on a happy day for you children. If you will keep still we will see Mvuu, when he rises."

We froze in our tracks, and peering through the undergrowth, had not long to wait before we saw two little ears, and then the nostrils, appear above the water.

He must have signalled that all was well, for he was shortly followed by Mrs. Hippo with, COULD WE BELIEVE OUR EYES? Yes, it was true: a round, and rather pink little baby perched on her broad back!

We scarcely dared to breathe, as we watched the happy family party for a full five minutes. Then a pair of excited "Hammer-heads"* flew overhead giving their harsh cry of warning and Pa, Ma and their baby sank silently from our view.

"Bother those horrid Hammer-heads," we exclaimed as one. We knew that it would be useless to wait in the hopes of seeing them again; all wild animals have a great respect for the Hammer-head's warning, so we lost no time in preparing our mid-day meal.

*Hammer-head – Scopus umbretta bannermani.
Matabele – Tegwani.

Chakuti commenced to pluck the three fat wood-pigeons that had fallen to Farewell's good aim earlier that morning, and we hastened to gather wood for a fire.

We were literally "as hungry as hunters", and soon the birds were sizzling on their spits over the open fire. How good they smelled – and how good they tasted, as we sat, with our backs to a fallen tree trunk, picking their bones, and going over the morning's happenings.

"Chakuti, what about our story? What have you to tell us to-day?" I asked. "Tell us about Mvuu. Tell us how the people who live by the big rivers hunt the tribe of Mvuu in their canoes."

"Ah yes," agreed Chakuti, as he squatted on his haunches and poked our dying fire into a blaze. "But you see, Mvuu has not always been a water animal. Our ancestors used to hunt him in the forests, and snare him in pits set along the game paths. But to-day it is more difficult, because the prey that you can see is ever more easy to come by, than the one that hides beneath the water. Now, it is only the dwellers by the big rivers and lakes who can lay in stores of his soft white fat, to make their porridge smooth and tasty, and to make their children grow strong."

"What do you mean?" broke in Farewell. "Mvuu is made like Xoxo the frog, to live both under the water and above. We all know that."

Chakuti shook his head. "That may be so *now*, but not when the Big Lord arranged His plans. In those days Mvuu was of great standing among the Forest People. He was much looked up to for his beauty."

"But who can call Mvuu beautiful?" I laughed.

"Listen," he said, "and I will tell you."

And so he commenced:

*

Amidst the forest-lands of Zimbabwe, in the years gone by, there lived a large and hairy creature. To us, to-day, he would be known as "Mvuu" (the hippopotamus). In those days he lived as the other creatures lived, among the forest-lands. He was the possessor of a very fine coat of nut-brown hair, of which he was extremely proud.

With bushy tail waving grandly, regularly at noon-time he would take his daily stroll to the river for his mid-day drink. He nodded and chatted to all the creatures whom he met on the way, and day after day he would ask them if they did not consider that his was the most beautiful coat and tail in the forest?

The monkeys in the treetops, with their foolish little addle-pates always agreed with anything if they heard it often enough, and would answer in chorus:

"Well said, oh noble friend; great is your beauty; strong are your limbs, and luscious is your silky brown hair. Justified is your pride. Oh! exquisite, beautiful one."

They would throw garlands of creepers from the treetops, and these he would wear round his foolish neck, as he drank in their flattery and their praise.

Day by day his vanity increased, until it became clear to the forest dwellers that he would become completely insufferable, if he was not taken down a peg or two.

After a long and deep drink he would sit at the side of his favourite pool, and gaze with joy at the reflection in the water of his beautiful hairy image.

Now, this was nobody's business but his own, but he brought about his downfall by not keeping his very large mouth shut.

"Ha-ha-ha," he would laugh as he sat there, "The nkau (monkeys) are right. I certainly have decent-sized ears; a decent-sized tail; legs of a decent length, and a *beautiful* figure. Not like that foolish Vundhla, who has a ridiculously small tail; foolishly long ears; completely unbalanced legs, and what a starved little body!"

Unfortunately for the hippo, the hare's long ears repeatedly caught the sound of the hearty laughter, and the belittling remarks about him. These remarks annoyed him more and more, until one day he could stand it no longer, and decided to set about teaching this rude fellow a lesson.

With very great cunning he commenced to make his plans. First he laid in a store of tinder-dry grass. This he carried and stacked in a big circle around the patch of forest in which the hippo had made his sleeping quarters.

"What are you doing that for?" the hippo suspiciously asked when he saw the hare putting a large armful in place one evening.

"Well, winter is nearly upon us," answered the hare, "and I thought that a wall of this grass around your sleeping quarters would keep the cold wind from ruffling your beautiful coat."

"Very thoughtful of you," agreed the hippo, "of course a coat and tail as beautiful as mine should, in the interests of everybody, be protected against ALL bad weather. I am glad to know that you realise your responsibilities. Good night," and he settled down with a yawn.

Now the hare went away smarting with rage and fury, but looking very smug and purposeful as he muttered to himself, "Just you wait, my friend!"

His first stop was at an African village up a hill nearby, in a little clearing. Here he hid himself among the brushwood that formed part of the goat kraal. Soon he saw the people gather around the evening pot of food, while the village dogs waited expectantly for the porridge scrapings.

"This is my chance!" purred the hare as, with a hop, skip and a jump, he made for the door-way of the nearest hut. Yes, he was lucky. Just what he wanted.

There was a smouldering fire in the middle of the hut and, joy of joys, a broken clay pot was lying nearby. He carefully selected two bits of broken pot, and clapped a glowing piece of wood between them. With these tucked safely under his arm, he made all speed for the forest.

With great care, so as not to put out the precious embers that he was carrying, he crept to the hippo's resting place. With equal care, he set fire at many points, to the circle of dry grass that he had so carefully laid. There was a soft breeze blowing, and soon a loud crackling began.

With a grunt and a roar the hippo woke up, and dashed wildly from side to side, only to be met at each turn by the tall licking flames.

At last he was pressed to the very centre of his bower, and there the flames caught his beautiful nut-brown coat. Like a ball of flame, he rushed through the now blazing forest, and into his favourite pool he plunged, just in time to save his life.

With terror in his heart, he stayed under the water for as long as his breath lasted.

When his lungs were close to bursting, he rose to the surface, putting only his eyes and his nose above the water. But he ducked down again in haste, as the hot breath from the fire seared his burnt nose and face.

From time to time he rose to the surface; but he felt safer under the soft, soothing, friendly water. Before long he became quite used to staying for long periods under-water, and he commenced to browse on the juicy plants that he found on the river bed.

In time, when the fire had died down, and the hissing and the crackling had ceased, he ventured to crawl out onto the bank.

He was very stiff and sore; but he was alive! He could almost afford to laugh at the hare for his clumsy knavery.

But could he? What was that?

He had caught sight of himself in the mirror of the pool from which he had just emerged. Could he believe his eyes? What were those silly little blobs where his silky ears had been? All the hair gone, and the edges frizzled away? No wonder they had been so painful!

He turned to look at his lovely tail. Not a hair left on either it, or his bare grey body.

In shame he hastily returned to the pool once more. As he sank out of sight, he breathed all the air out of his body, so that he would sink the easier, and the noise was as though he had said "MVUU"; and for ever after, that has been his name.

And thus he has spent his days, leaving only his eyes and his nose above the water, lest the animals that had known him in his glory, should laugh at him in his shame.

From that day to this, Mvuu has been a creature of the rivers and lakes, coming out of the water only at night time to walk and to graze on the fringes of the forest.

Farewell and I sat up with a start. We had been carried to another world by Chakuti's strange story.

"Poor Mvuu," I sighed. "No wonder he is so shy. Yes, Chakuti, that was a good story. It is late, we must now hurry home!"

THE HONEY-GUIDE'S REVENGE

It was honey-time. During most of the year there was honey in the hollows of the trees, or sometimes in the holes in the ground. But the best time of all was when the combs were full to overflowing, and the fat little bee grubs were close to hatching.

At such times the persistent little brown honey-guides (*Prodotiscus insignis zambesiae*) sought us out, and compelled us to follow them kilometres through the bush, to the honey-store.

Bee grubs are the favourite food of these little birds, and instinct tells them that only by the hand of man can they feast on this juicy white delicacy.

Therefore, close to the time when these grubs are "ripe", the honey-guide searches out human beings, both Black and White, and with its persistent call of "che-che-che", it flies from tree to tree, compelling the humans to follow. It finally guides them to the honey-store.

One day, while on our rambles, Farewell and I had found a little night ape's home in a hole high up in a big tree on a koppie nearby, and had begged Lee to spare the old wagon driver to help us to capture the tiny creature, for a much desired pet.

With hopes running high the three of us set out, in single file as usual, swinging down the path that zig-zagged through the bush, and were soon lost to sight in the masasa* trees.

We must have been half way to our objective when, from a tree above us burst an excited "che-che-che" – a pause, then a more urgent "che-che-che", and there swooped past us, almost touching our ears, a very excited little honey-guide.

He flew straight on, perching on a tree about fifty metres ahead while he continued his chatter.

"Honey!" we exclaimed as one. "Let us follow Sedhlu."

After all, we could come for the night-ape another day; but would we find Sedhlu again? We decided to look for the honey. Chakuti was full of enthusiasm. Had he not brought an axe and a box in which we had hoped to put the night-ape? This box would hold a *lot* of honey! He smacked his lips in anticipation (so, I must admit, did we!).

No sooner had Sedhlu realised that we understood his antics, than he almost burst his little throat with excitement, flitting from tree to tree, and simply chattering with joy.

Finally, after following him for about a kilometre, he came to rest in a large yellow-wood tree. Here he changed his tune to a gentle twittering, and flitted from branch to branch, darting frequently towards a small hole in the tree.

"Ah," said Chakuti, "our walk has ended. His lordship speaks in a different voice," and there, sure enough, were the bees flying in and out of the hole in the tree trunk.

Sedhlu then flitted gracefully to another tree about twenty metres away, fluffed his feathers, put his little head on one side, and settled down to watch us, and wait for his reward, as much as to say, "there, I have done my share of the work, now do yours."

*Masasa, the tree of which most of the Zimbabwean bushveld is composed.

Very often a tree that is hollow half-way up, continues its hollowness right down to the ground, and this great yellow-wood tree was not an exception.

We soon found a gaping hole at its base, and in front of this we built a fire. When it was blazing merrily, we piled on to it a large armful of green leaves, which produced clouds of thick white smoke, which we carefully fanned into the hole behind it.

As the smoke rose up the tunnel inside the tree, an angry buzzing could be heard – but this soon changed to a contented humming as the bees became stupefied, and we knew that we would have no trouble from our sharp-tailed friends.

In no time Chakuti had climbed the tree and chopped away a big square piece of the old trunk, exposing a large cavern filled with dripping combs. These he proceeded to hand down to us, and we packed them into the night-ape box.

"What we cannot carry home, we will eat," he called out gleefully, as he passed us the last comb.

Little Sedhlu grew more and more excited as Chakuti climbed down, and he watched with unconcealed impatience as he saw a large piece, full of fat white bee-grubs put aside for him.

"Always put it thus, Nkosizana," said Chakuti, as he placed a branch over the bee grubs, half hiding them from view.

"But why hide them, when Sedhlu watches what you do?" I laughed.

"Well, you see, Nkosizana," answered Chakuti, "Sedhlu eats but a little at a time, for his crop is small. The hot sun scorches and dries up the juicy grubs. Shaded they last for many days, and it is good to provide for his wants ahead. It happened once, that one he called, failed to reward him for his pains. Still to this day, is the punishment of the guilty one talked of among our people."

"Tell us, Chakuti, of how Sedhlu punished the greedy one," we begged.

Now, the thoughtful honey robber will never sit down straight away to commence on his own feast. This is asking too much of Sedhlu's patience; so we carried our load to a tree some fifty metres away, and there we sat licking our dripping fingers, and breaking off sticky chunks of comb for our own enjoyment.

When we had eaten our fill, Chakuti leaned against the tree trunk and said:

Children, there are some who have greed in their hearts from the time they take their mother's breasts, and it happened that one day Sedhlu met a man of this kind, and trustingly took him to his honey-store.

But Ncitjana (the mean one) had no thought for his feathered guide. His only thoughts were for his own belly, and he scraped from the trunk, even the honey drops that had fallen as he worked.

Nothing did he leave for Sedhlu, and sorrowfully the little bird hopped about on the ground beneath the tree. Carefully he searched, lest perchance Ncitjana had left *something* hidden *somewhere*. But not a honey drop, nor a bee grub did he find.

A great rage then seized Sedhlu, and he vowed that he would punish the greedy one.

He searched the bush for many days, and in time his search was rewarded. He found a fierce mother leopard, with her two spotted babies, well concealed in a hollow, beneath a fallen tree trunk, and off in glee he flew.

Straight to Ncitjana's kraal he went, and there he sought him out from all the rest, diving low past his head. So that no one else would hear, he gave his call close to the ear, "che-che-che".

Ncitjana slipped away, so that none should share his prize, telling none of his plans, the better to be able to eat his fill.

Kilometre after kilometre he followed Sedhlu, singing as he went the Honey Song,

> "Quiri ra makuti, makuti, makuti, – den den den,
> Tsa-tsaga-tsa, gwarang-ga, quiri-ra."

thus the honey badger sings whilst he shakes the bees from his bristly head, as he robs the hive. Until, right above the leopard's lair Sedhlu perched, and there he changed his tune.

"Ah," said Ncitjana, "my walk ends here," and he stepped on the fallen trunk, the easier to climb the tree that rose above him.

As you know, children, "The Spotted One" looks as the shadows amongst which she lives, and Ncitjana's foot was almost on a spotted cub, when, with a savage snarl, the angry mother sprang.

Who, with his bare hands, can fight "The Spotted One", when she de-

fends her young? Ncitjana's end was as swift as it was terrible; Sedhlu's revenge was sweet.

*

"So, White Children, revenge comes not only from us who talk, but from The Great Lord's dumb creatures too.
   No one now, will cheat Sedhlu."

4

THE DEATH OF THE CHAMELEON

One hot day, the oxen had been outspanned for their mid-day break on the river bank. Farewell and I were leaning against the wagon wheel munching our sandwiches, when we saw a large chameleon, tail erect, gaily stepping across the road.

We were watching its progress when, before we could intervene, Chakuti appeared from seemingly nowhere, and seized it by the tail.

The chameleon turned, as they do, in anger, with mouth opened wide, to hiss. Quick as a flash, he threw something into its open mouth – and we went to investigate.

"Do not worry," said Chakuti in a tone of finality, "it will soon be dead."

"Dead?" I cried. "What have you done? It is my friend. I do not want it killed."

"Yes, I know it is your friend," he answered sullenly. "But do not scold me for killing my ENEMY. The race of the 'Hamba Kahle' (careful walker) has done us Black people great harm. To punish them for this harm we MUST kill them always, when we see them"

"What have you given to my friend?" I cried, holding the writhing body in my two hands, tears fast splashing down on him. "We must save him!"

"You cannot save him," he muttered, squatting down on his heels opposite to us. "Snuff works quickly on such as these. It is done. He will do no more harm to my tribe."

"What harm," broke in Farewell, "could such a small thing do, to a tribe as big and as strong as yours? You talk as a fool – or a coward."

"A fool?" he asked. "But of course you White people do not understand." He shook his head, and gazed down at his feet, as he traced strange shapes in the dust of the road with his finger. "A coward, you say? My spear has drunk deep of the blood of the Mighty One, the lion. Can I be judged, then, a coward?"

After a pause he continued, "It is all the fault of the Slow Walker that we have remained black throughout the ages."

"How can you say such a thing?" I questioned. "How can so small a creature cause such a big matter to a tribe?"

"Listen, White Children, and I will tell you. You will then know why we must always kill 'your friend', there is time enough, for the oxen still eat, and they pull the better on a full belly."

*

It happened a very long time ago, when the Big Lord of the Heavens was still completing His plans. All people were then Black, and lacking in much wisdom.

One day He thought that it would be good to make all people White and possessed of great knowledge. He therefore commanded one of the rivers to come down in spate. He sent messengers from the Animal, Reptile and Insect Kingdoms to call all the human tribes from far and near; bidding them to pass through, and drink of this heavenly liquid, and thereby they would become White, and absorb great knowledge –

To one tribe He sent the Monkey. To another He sent the noble Lion; to yet another He sent the Jackal – all fleet of foot, and obedient. The Lizard too, was not forgotten, and as you know, his speed is great. There are many tribes, as there are many creatures.

It came at last to the lot of the Chameleon, that "Slow Walker" to take the order to the tribe of my ancestors. For many moons the "Slow One" put one foot before the other, then pulled it back to ponder once more whether forwards or backwards. Two, three and four times before finally his step was taken – with great meditation of "this" and "that".

It happened that when at last he had delivered his message to our leader, and the tribe rushed down in obedience, to the river, they beheld nothing but the dry river bed.

The spate had long since passed, and there remained but the damp sand, where the water had once been. Enough to damp only the soles of our feet, and the palms of our hands. These parts of our bodies you will see ARE white.

My people kissed the damp sands with their lips, in the effort to drink of this knowledge. But wisdom did not enter this way. There was no water left, beneath which to dip their bodies. They even sucked the damp pebbles, but little moisture did they get, beyond the sweet taste, which gave them the desire for MORE of these Waters of Knowledge. But the Heavenly Wisdom eluded us. The taste dried on our tongues as we searched for it. Do you wonder that we have no love for the "Slow Walker"?

*

The little form in my hands stiffened, and was still. I rose, with tear rimmed eyes, and carried it carefully to add yet another grave to my strange little cemetery.

5

THE TALE OF NGCEDE,
THE SPOTTED CLOUD WARBLER

One glorious September morning we inspanned the wagon and went camping, the Roberts family and ourselves, and as we sat, weary after the day's hunting one starlit evening, we heard a discussion among the camp hands as they sat around the fire cooking their evening meal.

As Farewell and I were always ready for a tale, we edged our way into the circle in time to hear Chakuti say,

"Yes, Ngcede IS a great Chief, and wise beyond all birds."

"Why do you say that?" I asked, "for surely he is the smallest of all God's feathered things!"

"Because, children," he replied, turning to Farewell and myself, "his cleverness is known to all; for surely it is a great thing for one so small as he, to be made Chief of a family as large as our friends the birds! Now look at the size of the ostrich, yet even *he* has to bow his long neck to Ngcede!"

There was a ripple of laughter round the fire, and I asked:

"But what cause could there be for such a silly thing?"

*

It was a long time ago, before the Great Lord had given the beasts, birds and insects, their status upon the earth; and there was quarrelling, and ill-doing among His Feathered Children.

One day He thought that it would be good to make a Chief among the feathered things: one with wisdom and cunning, who could advise those in his care, on matters of importance, and keep the peace among the Feathered People. He therefore called all those concerned to a conclave, and told them of His plan.

"Tomorrow at noon," He said, "when the sun has reached the highest part of Heaven, all must gather on the big open grasslands, and when I give the signal, all must fly straight up to Me. The first one to touch My outstretched Hand, *his* kind will be Chief of all Feathered things, and all must obey his commands."

There was much excitement among the Bird People. The ambitious ones preened their feathers, and checked on their wing-spans.

The great eagle, Kosi, looked proudly at his strong muscles, and stretched his wings to their full extent, so that all could see their power. Such wings would never tire, and, over such a distance, surely none could fly against him?

A cruel glint came into his large yellow eyes, as he thought of the plan that he would follow; while all the Feathered People around him trembled, and thought of the safety of the dense forests.

All, that is, except little Ngcede, but whoever noticed Ngcede? He was much too small to notice. With bright little eyes aglitter, he hopped about as cockily as ever, with his ridiculously tiny tail even higher than usual. No dense forests for *him*. He knew that he was quick enough to avoid the cruel strike of Kosi's wicked beak. He nodded his wise little head, and went about his business.

The next day at noon, when the sun had reached the required height, it found all the birds gathered anxiously on the Great Plain. The sign came in the form of a great clap of thunder, and the vast feathered multitude rose into the sky.

Still no one thought of Ngcede – least of all Kosi, the Mighty One. But the tiny bird was *very much* there, and as Kosi spread his wings to rise, Ngcede shot like a little arrow, on to the mighty one's shoulder, and there he clung.

The big eagle felt a slight disturbance of his feathers, and shook himself, to dislodge the troublesome "fly", with an exclamation of "Heyi, suka" (here get away!). But the "fly" clung on, and Kosi did not worry any more, but settled down to his long flight.

Higher and higher the great flight rose, far out of sight of the wide plains below. Slower and slower the long ascent, as the bodies dragged on the tiring wings.

Not so Kosi; his powerful wings drove him upward, untiring, determined.

One by one the others fell behind. Some gave up entirely; others struggled on – but Kosi led them all.

Finally he was the only one left in the great race. At least he *thought* he was, so he slackened his speed, and rested for a while, almost stationary, as these big birds do, before they swoop.

Only a few more yards to go. He could afford to take it easy. But what was that? His eye caught sight of little Ngcede, shooting like a streak of lightning from his shoulder, straight into the very gates of Heaven, and into the outstretched Hand!

*

"Do not such brains deserve to lead the Feathered Ones?" asked the old wagon driver as he smiled on the circle of his listeners.

6

BROTHER TO THE RAT

It was not long after our episode with the honey-guide, that the wild pigs, always wicked raiders of the mealie lands, gave us more attention than usual. As they did their raiding by night, they were not easy thieves to shoot. Lee therefore detailed Chakuti to dig a game pit in the bush, along the path that led to the mealie fields.

Of course Farewell and I looked upon this as a great occasion, and accompanied the old wagon driver on his task. We first examined the field to which the greatest damage had been done, to find the path by which the pigs travelled to their midnight feasts.

Soon we had found a perfect place, where the path ran between two thorny thickets, too dense to pass on either side – and there we dug our pit. It was six feet deep, with sloping sides that formed a V, so that when Ngulube (the pig) fell into it, his feet would have no grip to make a jump, and so allow him to escape.

Once the oblong hole was dug, we covered it carefully with thin and brittle saplings. On these we laid a covering of leaves, and capped it all with a sprinkling of earth.

The saplings could hold the leaves and earth, but no more, so that when Ngulube passed that way, unless his instinct saved him, his capture was almost sure.

It was tedious work, and so deeply intent were we on our task, that we failed to notice the sudden dark stillness that had closed in around us, and our first realisation of a storm was large solitary drops of rain, and a deep roll of thunder. .

"Quickly, Children," exclaimed Chakuti, "we have worked too long. The Lord of the Heavens walks abroad. Do you not hear His footsteps?" as another rumble of thunder shook the earth. "We can reach the cave in the big rocks in time, if we hurry," and we made all speed for our refuge.

We had soon reached the low entrance to the cave, and, to make sure that "The Spotted One" (the leopard) had not taken refuge there before us, we threw in several stones, calling from the threshold, in the african fashion, "Are you there, My Lord of the Spots?"

There was a flurry of bats from the darkness within, but nothing else so we crept into the dry cavern, as the clouds above opened wide to pour down their contents in sheets of rain.

"Like our friend Sedhlu," I cried, as the bats flew past our heads, almost touching us, as they made their exit.

"That is why some call them 'Duzi Ndhlebe'," (close to the ear) said Chakuti, "for thus flies Sedhlu, and it is well known that long ago the Bat and the Bird People were one. In the past the bat had feathers, as do all the bird tribe."

"But Chakuti," broke in Farewell, "who has heard of one of the bird tribe who gives birth to her young, and suckles them?"

"This I know," pondered the old man, "and yet, who has heard of the animal that flies? It has been handed down among my people that, in the time of which I speak, before the Great Drought struck both bird and beast, the bat WAS a feathered creature."

"Tell us, Chakuti, of Lulwane (the bat), and of how he lost his feathers!" we begged.

"Well there is time to be passed, for the storm has but commenced. However, my clothes are few, Nkosana,* and I shiver, for there is no warmth in this underground hole. A fire, and some snuff would unfreeze my memory, for this tale was told to me before I was of an age to herd my father's goats."

We gathered some dry wood from the floor of the cave, with which we built a little fire, and soon the air became heavy with its smoke – but the old man's eyes were used to the permanent smoke of his hut, and he said with a smile:

"Already, Nkosana, does my tongue feel loosened. Let me take a pinch of snuff, and I will look back through the smoke."

He sat on his haunches for a while, with his hands spread out to catch the warmth of the little blaze, and then he commenced.

*

It has been handed down by my ancestors, that before the Big Drought struck, Lulwane the bat had his place among the Bird People. He was looked up to by reason of the beauty of his many-coloured feathers. But

*Young master.

those who *liked* him were few, for his greed and his selfishness were known to all.

Never would he share his feeding grounds with others in times of shortage, but would leave the tree roosts while it was still dark, so that none should see him go. And then came the Big Drought.

As the months wore on, and still no rain fell to swell the hard dry fruit, or fill the failing pools, Lulwane (sleek and fat, whilst others starved) was driven from his kind by reason of his greed, and took refuge in a cave.

Earlier and earlier he commenced his furtive trips to his food store. His flights were swift almost as the eye can travel, and he tarried not on the way, for he no longer wished to meet his kind.

Soon his eyesight became as those who see-by-night, and by day he lived in caves and in dark places, where he could rest undisturbed, and the sun would not hurt his eyes.

But although his secret food store filled his eating needs, water he could not find. And of what good is food, when there is no water to make the blood run? Dew there was, that fell by night – but this rolled off the leaves before his beak could even wet its tip. All beasts and birds were in a sorry state.

Now, one tribe amongst the rest, had brains beyond the others; that of Gundwane, the rat. Besides brains, they also had hands; and who is afraid to work when his throat is dry?

It therefore came about that the Rat People combined to smooth out a large and gently sloping basin in the earth, and to pound it well with small clenched fists. To this, they worked in clay from the deeper water-holes, (the bottoms of which were still damp) thus to catch and hold the dew that nightly eluded them.

With deft and careful hands, the great multitude of Rat People built a Dew Pond. Some carried the clay; others carefully worked it into the dry and crumbling earth.

Soon their task was done, and no longer did the precious dew sink from sight, but slowly trickled down the sloping sides, and gathered in a liquid pool for all to drink.

Great was the rejoicing among both birds and beasts. Long was the procession that gathered at dawn each day, to slake their thirsts. Loud were the praises of the clever rat.

"Now," said Lulwane, "will I leave my kind forever, and become as the

rat; for who among the Bird People could have provided water to quench the thirsts of all? Surely Gundwane has brains and skill beyond the rest!"

Therefore did Lulwane come earlier and earlier to slake his thirst; he came when it was still dark, and drank when the Rat People drank. Night by night he grew more like them, both in looks and voice, as he crept about amongst them around the water's edge.

But in some, habits of the ages cling; the rats returned to their holes in the ground, and there they spent the daylight hours. This Lulwane could not do; always he flew away as the first light greeted the day, and he sought the refuge of caves and dark places.

As he found no bough on which to perch within these caves, he clutched the roof, and there he hung upside down, and thus he sleeps today.

In time, through long absence from the sun, his many-coloured feathers failed in growth, and in the brilliance of their hue. Shorter and shorter the sun-starved feathers grew; duller and duller, until they had reached a dingy grey.

To protect him from the cold that dwells within the caves there grew instead, a covering of fur; his wings grew webbed, and his beak grew short, to form the mouth you see today. But still he flies with speed, close to the ear as does Sedhlu, when he calls you to his honey-find.

So, you see children, he WAS a bird. Who is there who can deny it?

*

We sat up with a start, to see the sunshine streaming in at the entrance to the cave, and realised that we, too, would welcome a coat of fur! And so we stepped out into the warmth and brilliance that followed the storm, and went back to repair any damage that the rain might have caused to our game pit.

7

THE HARE OUTWITS THE LION

A veld fire had been raging throughout the day. All hands, with sacks or green branches, had been trying to keep it from the hay fields.

The worst part of it seemed to be well under control, and three out of four of the haystacks were safe. The fourth was nearly safe when, as sometimes happens, the direction of the wind changed, and before we could get to the danger spot, a hungry tongue of flame had raced over the space between us and the stack, and with a crackle of joy, licked up the side of the tall haystack.

It was too late for us to save it, and we were too exhausted to look for more trouble. The rest of the beaters, with my brother, were on another part of the farm, and from where we stood all signs of fire from that quarter had ceased.

We sat down, to recover our breath – the three beaters, Chakuti and I, watching the tall flames envelope the stack, and the billows of smoke curling up to the sky.

Birds were there in great numbers, as always happens where a fire rages, to catch the horde of insects that fly before the heat, or those with singed wings that are unable to escape.

The elegant black drongo swooped through the smoke, to rise with a grasshopper in her beak. The ever watchful kite struck at a squirrel, as he fled from the flames. A startled doe bounded into an open clearing, and, with heaving sides, turned back her head with great ears spread, to catch the dread crackling of the flames.

With easy lopes a hare appeared from the long grass in an unburned patch – but somehow he seemed unhurried and not so distressed as the others, for he paused, and without a backward look, carefully washed his face with his two paws.

"See," said Chakuti, "Vundhla has little fear. He is wise in the ways of fires. Soon he will scoff at those who flee. Later, when all are weary with running from the terror, and the danger has passed, he will come up from behind, sleek, and laughing at their heaving sides!"

"But how can he return through the flames and not a hair of his coat be singed?" I asked as, sure enough, Vundhla loped to an ant-heap that was encircled by the fire, and was seen no more.

"It is, he will tell the others, because of the 'Muti' (medicine) given to him by Mpisi the hyena, who is well-known to be clever in the ways of magic, that the flames have no power to harm him."

"Tell me, Chakuti, of Mpisi's magic," I begged.

"It was when, as a child, I herded cattle on a 'ranchie' by the big Zambesi River, many weeks by road from where we sit, that I heard of this matter. Thus, in these words, was it told to me."

*

An angry fire was raging across the plains near the Zambesi River, and well had it bitten into the forest lands adjoining the open portion.

The tinder-dry grass was taller than the height of a man in many parts, and mighty was the racing demon of fire, which ate it up for miles on either side.

The wind was high, that drove the flames along. All living things were straining every limb to keep beyond the heat.

Elephant, lion, leopard, giraffe, cheetah – all buck and wild things ran together in a race to save their lives. With the big danger following, they showed no fear, each for the other, as they headed for the bush and tree-covered ground, where the speed and the heat of the flames would be less fierce.

At one point the fire had curved its horns to left and right, and almost joined in front. In the centre Silwana the lion had missed his wife and cubs. He turned to see if they were safe; but he hesitated just too long, and the two horns met in front of him.

He was trapped, and well he knew it. However, there was a narrow space to the side where the grass grew shorter and more sparsely on the hard baked clay. He had decided to risk a break-through there, when he heard a squeak from an ant-heap nearby.

It was Vundhla, the hare, who greeted him.

"Take it easy there, Uncle, take it easy. You will NEVER get through that way. Come to the shelter of this grassy ant-heap. No fire can touch us here. Did not the Witch Doctor, Mpisi, give me his BEST fire medicine only yesterday?"

Everybody had heard of Mpisi the hyena, and all had great faith in his medicines. He could move without a sound, and could not be seen, except when the sun was *very* bright. Surely, he was a *great* Witch Doctor! All the Veld People went to him for his charms.

This was luck indeed and Silwana was glad to accept Vundhla's kind offer, while the fire approached from all directions. He sat down with a sigh of relief – but sprang to his four feet again, as he glanced aside, to see Vundhla disappearing down an ant-bear hole, and heard a burst of foolish laughter coming up from deep down in the earth below him.

"So *that* was Vundhla's game!" he roared, as with a mighty leap through the licking flames he managed to make the burnt area on the other side.

But what a sorry-looking lion! The flames had caught his big bushy mane, which was his great pride! Eyebrows and whiskers burnt off! And the beautiful black tuft of hair at the end of his tail, completely gone! All this, just because he had allowed himself to be tricked by Vundhla, the Clown.

It would be months before he could once more walk with pride amongst the other animals. He made a vow that he would get even with Mr. Vundhla.

Well, two months had passed, and Silwana's coat looked a great deal better, though it had not reached its full length and warmth. He still felt rather naked and cold, when one day he was caught in a heavy shower of rain.

He bounded with haste to a near-by stony koppie, where he knew of a small, snug cave, in which he would be out of the rain, and could have a nice quiet sleep until the storm was over.

Arrived at the cave, he stood in the entrance, shaking the water from his ears, and looked around.

Could his eyes be deceiving him? There in a corner, trying to make himself invisible like Mpisi, stood Vundhla. His long ears were drooped with fear, and in spite of the warmth of the cave, he shivered. Well did he know that he had no cause to expect mercy from Silwana, who licked his lips and said:

"Well, Vundhla, I have got you where I want you at last! And I have waited quite a long time to get even with you. You made all the animals laugh at me during the last two months. Now, in a very short while, they will know what happened to YOU, and *you* will be the one they laugh at then!

"You are too small to make a meal for me – but you should taste good!"

He flicked his tail first to one side, and then to the other. As he spoke the noise of the rain stopped suddenly, and Silwana turned his head to see the sun burst forth from beneath a cloud.

As he did so, the hare, quick as the eye can travel, jumped across to a low hanging portion of the roof of the cave, where he pretended to hold up the rock, shouting:

"Uncle, Uncle, the cave is falling in. Please come and help me to hold it up. Come quickly, or we will both be crushed."

Silwana covered the distance in one bound, and placed his big paws against the rocky roof, and the pair pushed upwards with all their strength, until after a time the hare spoke again.

"Uncle, my arms are thinner than yours, and not so strong. They are very sore and tired. Let me collect some rocks to build a pillar to the roof, to ease your arms and mine; then we can both sit down and rest. Please hold the roof up while I get the rocks," and he vanished through the mouth of the cave.

When a long time had passed, and Vundhla had not returned with the stones, Silwana began to think that he had once more been tricked. He thereupon stopped pushing against the roof, and jumped backwards, landing well beyond the opening of the cave.

Nothing happened, and the roof still stayed up. Soon he *knew* that he had been tricked again, and a rumbling growl of anger came from deep down in his throat.

The sun was shining brightly after the storm, and presently he again heard a burst of foolish laughter, and the hare shouted:

"Uncle, what are you having for breakfast to-day?"

*

"So you see, Nkosizana, it is not the medicine of Mpisi that saves Vundhla from the fires, it is the holes of the ant bear. But it was his brain that saved him the second time! Well is he named 'The Clever One of the Veld'. Only once that I know has the laugh been against him."

However, no amount of begging or bribing would persuade Chakuti to tell me more, so we stretched our limbs after our long rest, and wended our way back home over the charred and still smoking veld.

8

THE DOWNFALL OF XOXO THE FROG

Dear little songster frogs visited us in the summer, and these we came to love. They were pretty, gentle, tiny little tree frogs, mostly fawn, or putty-coloured – though sometimes white and semi-transparent. They had large sticky fingers, and friendly natures, and they would sing as though their little throats would burst. Sometimes they would come right inside our huts, singing and whistling to us from the rafters.

There they would consume quantities of mosquitoes. Needless to say, they were most welcome visitors.

One had lived for many weeks in amongst the pink blooms of a lovely antigonon creeper, that grew over an arch in front of our verandah door.

Whether it had taken on the colour of the flowers, or whether it had come into the world delicately shaded with pink, I do not know, but it was exquisitely beautiful.

We learned to look forward to its evening song, as we sat on the verandah in the cool of the evening, after the day's work was done.

One evening, our little friend's song was interrupted by a long-drawn-out scream, and I rushed to see what ailed him.

By the light of a lamp carried in my hand, I was horrified to see our little songster being swallowed by a long green snake.

We hastily killed the snake, and rescued the frog from it's jaws – but we were too late – the little thing died in my hands.

There were other frogs too; bull-frogs, which were much more frightening fellows. These were great big monsters, that also appeared with the rains, and feasted on the flying-ants as they left their nests on their mating flights, after the first rains.

Their voices were harsh and powerful, and they were mostly head, with big sharp teeth, and vicious natures, attacking any stick that was poked at them.

There were harmless little round toads too, that foregathered at the flying-ants' Marriage Flights. On the slightest provocation they would puff themselves up to an enormous size – completely round – and nearly as big as a tennis ball. They would then waddle along, full of importance, in the most ridiculous manner.

They too, would choose a flying-ant's exit hole, and there they would sit, gorging on the ants as they came out to commence their flight. These Marriage Flights take place early in the rainy season, usually in the late afternoon. The male and female ants rise in their thousands, either from an ant-heap or from a small hole in the ground. Although they are known throughout the country as "white-ants" they are, actually, termites. They fly upwards, to mate in the air, returning to earth where they shed their gauzy wings and (those that have been lucky enough to survive) commence to build a new home.

Birds (especially the Black Drongo) and Africans, besides the frogs, attended these Marriage Flights.

The African women brought large handleless baskets made from grass, and these they would place over the holes, also intent on capturing this much-prized delicacy, as it reached the surface.

One evening Farewell and I were gazing, fascinated, at the fat little toads and frogs eating their fill as the ants came out. Several women had arrived with their basket traps, bringing their small children with them, and were popping the fat creamy little termite bodies into their mouths. Farewell and I joined them at their feast. No worse than eating oysters straight from the sea, surely? And even more tasty.

Some of the farm workers wandered down to join us, and Chakuti, who always had his finger in every pie (also with an eye to his supper), handed a gourd to one of the women to fill from her trap.

I was fondling a very round little frog at the time, and his eye fell on me. His jaw dropped in speechless horror, and he beat a hasty retreat.

"Ayi, Nkosizana," he called as he fled, "you touch Xoxo? Surely you will die!"

"Why should I die?" I laughed. "Xoxo and I have always been friends. See, I will show you his mouth. His teeth are too small to even see. How do you think he could bite, with such a harmless mouth?" and I carried the little creature towards him. "Come, I will show you."

There were shrieks from the women, followed by a stampede of black legs, and Farewell and I were left alone with our laughter.

It was a long time before they would re-join us. Only when we promised that we would not touch Xoxo again.

Darkness was coming down upon us, and it was difficult to see to catch any more flying-ants, so we accompanied the men back to their huts, where a great cooking and sizzling took place.

When all had eaten, and the blue smoke was spiralling up to the twinkling stars Farewell said, "Surely it was not a grown man whom I heard say that he was afraid of a small frog?"

Chakuti looked uneasy, and spat into the fire.

"Xoxo is a wicked one," he muttered, "all Black people will tell you this."

"But how is he bad?" I asked. "I have always played with him, and he has never harmed me."

"It was a long time ago," he commenced, "that he did his mischief. Nowhere among our people will you find one who will spare Xoxo when he comes upon him. But it grows late."

"Not too late to hear about the misdeeds of Xoxo, before the fire dies away?" we begged.

"Very well," he said, "those flying ants are sitting well on my stomach. I am suti (full), and at such times words fall easily from my lips."

Then, as we poked the fire into a cheerful blaze, our Story Teller began his tale.

*

Many, many moons ago, perhaps as many as you can count stars in the sky above us, there was a good and wise chief of our people. He was looked up to by all. Great was his happiness. His cattle were sleek and fat, and his grain stores were full to bursting.

His wives were fruitful, and great too, was his pride in his children. One child in particular was the apple of his eye – a young girl of fourteen summers.

She was beautiful beyond words, and full of laughter. She was loved by all. Soon she would bring her father further wealth, for her marriage-price was high. A comely Princess indeed. Already suitors had approached their ruler for her hand.

Daily, when the sun was hot, the children of the Royal Kraal played in the cool clear waters of the nearby river.

One day his beloved princess went as usual, with a friend, to play in the water.

"Let us go to another pool today," she said. "Just we two. Maybe we can find one where the water is cooler."

They went further up the river, to where they had never been before, to a pool of great beauty, and there they slipped into the crystal clear water.

The little fish were full of curiosity, and nibbled at the strange black legs. This caused laughter and merriment, while they splashed and enjoyed themselves.

There was someone, however, who was very far from pleased at their enjoyment. It was Xoxo, the frog. He sat on the edge of the pool, in his little house, *just* under the bank. As he sat there his head was slightly above the level of the water, and, feeling very full of song, he opened his mouth, and raised his voice in a magnificent croak – at least it was meant to be a magnificent croak – but it ended abruptly in a stupid gurgling noise.

A big wave had washed right into his open mouth and down his throat, completely drowning his song. Most annoying.

He waited until the water was calm again, then once more opened his mouth to let everyone within earshot hear exactly what a beautiful voice he had.

To his further great annoyance, exactly the same thing happened again, only this time, to make matters worse, he heard a titter of amusement from a tree nearby.

"Am I no longer King in my own pool, that I am to be disturbed in this manner?" he spluttered through the water. "Who dares to ruffle the water of my kingdom?"

There was no answer – but a few seconds later such a mighty wave came, that it washed him completely *out* of his little cave, and turned him right over onto his back.

In a state of tremendous rage now, he climbed out on to the bank and looked around him, until his gaze fell upon the little princess and her friend, disporting themselves in his pool.

"Oh!" he said, "now I see. It is YOU and *YOU*!"

He raised himself on his front legs and drew back his head, opening his mouth as he did so. First at one child, and then at the other, he shot out a cloud of wicked gas, whereupon they threw up their arms and died.

"Now, White Children, who is Xoxo that he should expect mercy from us?"

There was a dead silence around the dying fire. Then one by one, like shadows, the men slipped into their huts.

There was a rumble of thunder in the distance, and a great chorus of croaks burst upon the night, as the frogs in the vlei heralded the coming storm – and Farewell and I too, stole off to bed.

9

THE HEN AND THE MONGOOSE

Our pets brought sorrow to us as well as joy – for, as one of our Zimbabwean poets wrote: "There are tragedies that hover 'twixt the dawning and the day"; and night prowlers were a continual danger.

A little common hen was my companion and my joy. Her name was Penny. She was more like a dog than a feathered thing, for she followed me almost as loyally. She never failed to join us at our day-light meals, for she knew that many a scrap from my plate would find its way into her ever ready crop; she even accompanied me on my bicycle at times, tucked beneath my arm.

One day she disappeared, and I spent fruitless hours searching for her, calling her name from time to time. She came, however, in the end, racing to join the usual scramble when the bowl of grain was scattered in the poultry yard at feeding time.

She was full of importance, feathers ruffled, and clucking loudly; my hopes were confirmed. She had a nest hidden somewhere, and her brooding period had commenced. I followed her carefully, and she finally led me to a gooseberry bush, where I found ten eggs carefully hidden in a snug nest.

I felt that before long I would be the proud possessor af a batch of sturdy chickens. However, I learned only too soon the danger of "counting one's chickens before they are hatched", when one morning I found that poor little Penny had been killed by a night marauder. Her headless body lay not far from her cozy nest.

As I ran down the path that led to the house, with my lifeless pet in my arms, I met Chakuti.

"Eh! Nkosizana! what, has Bucagiti (the mongoose) taken her revenge once more?" he asked.

"Chakuti, why do you say that?" I sobbed. "What cause can Bucagiti have for revenge against one as harmless as my little hen? Such a gentle one as this could never cause trouble to a sharp-toothed mongoose!"

"It is the result of an ancient feud," he replied, "for Kukukazi the hen, caused Bucagiti to make herself the laughing-stock of all the creatures of the wild."

My curiosity checked my tears, and I said, "I must know about this. Feuds between feather and feather I can understand, but what could cause a feud between feather and fur?"

"They are of one race, the dumb creatures," answered the old African, "but the understanding between the *tribes*, is as between ourselves. Listen to the tale of Kukukazi and Bucagiti.

A long, long while ago there was good-fellowship and visiting between feather and fur. Some, as you know, turn night into day – and such it was with Bucagiti the mongoose. The Feathered People (except for the owl and his kind), prefer to sleep by night. Therefore when, from time to time Bucagiti made it his habit to call on Kukukazi and her lord as the dark was falling, for the friendly pot of beer, Makuti, the rooster, found great difficulty in remaining awake to entertain his night-loving guest.

On one such occasion he had already mounted to the cross beams of his hut and, with head tucked comfortably beneath his wing, as is the habit with the Bird People, he was both deaf and blind to all that passed beneath him, so deep was his slumber.

"Good evening, Kukukazi," said the Mongoose, as he poked his sharp nose into the rooster's hut; "I hear you have made a fresh brew of beer, and as I was passng with my wife and family, thought we would drop in to pass our opinion on it."

The hen was far from pleased at such a late visit, for she had, at that very minute, been on the point of joining her husband up aloft, to bury *her* head in the snugness of her feathers. Also, although there was an outward friendship between these two, Kukukazi had seen Mrs. Bucagiti licking her lips in a most suspicious manner on occasions when she came from the direction of Kukukazi's nest; and at times she thought her egg-count was not as she remembered from the day before. However, she was a polite little bird, so she hid her displeasure, and begged her guests to be seated, while she went to an adjoining hut to fetch them each a pot of beer.

While she was away, Mrs. Bucagiti's gaze travelled upwards, and there she saw, to her great amazement, the master of the hut, sitting on a beam up in the roof, apparently without a head! She could hardly contain her excitement, and as soon as the hen returned she pointed upwards and said, "My friend, what has happened to your husband's head?"

"Oh," replied the hen, "that is nothing. When evening comes I always chop it off, for then he sleeps more peacefully, and I am not awakened so early by his piercing crows. When the first rays of sunlight come in under the door, I put his head back again. It is easy; and the benefit is felt by all!"

Mrs. Bucagiti said nothing, but decided that she would not be outdone by this self-assured creature – so, after a few more pots of beer, and the usual pleasantries, the mongoose family took its leave, after a promise from the hen to return the call at noon on the following day.

As she flew up to join her husband, Kukukazi muttered, "*That* will give the egg-eating thief something to think about!" and, tucking her own head beneath her wing, was soon fast asleep.

Just before noon on the following day, the hen and her husband set out as arranged, for the mongoose's home, though before they had covered more than half the distance, they saw Mrs. Bucagiti racing down the path to meet them.

Without a word she seized the rooster by the neck, and commenced to move his head from side to side. "Yes," she muttered, "as firm as ever it was," and without another word she turned and rushed back to her hut.

The rooster and his wife were greatly intrigued, and followed her with haste through the doorway. There they found her with a blood-stained axe at her side, vainly trying to stick the heads on to the lifeless bodies of her husband and three children!

"Since that day the mongoose has never forgiven the hen. It is the memory of this happening that makes Mrs. Bucagiti take her revenge whenever chance comes her way. You see Nkosizana, it sometimes happens that a joke goes down the throat the wrong way, and none of us like to choke!"

10

A RACE BETWEEN THE TORTOISE AND THE HARE

One day I saw Chakuti going to his hut, with what looked very much like a tortoise in his hand. I ran after him to see what he had found.

Yes, a tortoise it was, and I well knew what the poor thing's fate would be!

"What are you going to do with Fudu?" I asked.

"You know, Nkosizana, what a good stew Fudu makes, with some of those hot, red chillies that grow by the door of my hut," he replied.

"Yes, but I think you could buy better meat than that when you take the wagon with the mealie bags to the town tomorrow, if I give you sixpence for Fudu. There is no fat inside Fudu, and if you ask the meat man for a fatty piece, think how well it will mix with the dryness of the mealie-meal!"

"Well yes," he agreed, "Fudu is yours for that much money. But what do *you* want with Fudu?"

"Fudu will have a hole made at the edge of his shell, and he will live at the end of a long rope. You know that these creatures are my friends," I replied.

He laughed at the thought of anyone making a friend of Fudu, and at the White race in general – but handed the tortoise over in great haste, in case I should change my mind, saying as he did so, "Fudu has great cunning in that snake-like head of his, for all his foolish looks. He is the only one I know who has tricked the smart Vundhla, and made him feel ashamed."

"Let me put my new child in a safe place, and I will come and hear how you can say this," I called over my shoulder, as I ran down the path to the house.

This was a good chance, I thought, to roast some green mealies, which are always nicer with the slightly acrid taste of the smoke and the glowing embers. So I made all haste back to the cook hut, and while my mealies were roasting in the embers, this is what I heard.

Fudu the tortoise was eating juicy bulb leaves near Ramba water-hole, which was surrounded by tall palm trees. He was enjoying his breakfast, and would soon close his doors and windows and go to sleep for the day. But as he decided to crawl into a clump of grass nearby, he heard the patter, patter of light feet, and there in front of him stood Vundhla, the hare.

"Good morning, Uncle," said Vundhla, "I'm sorry to disturb you, but I have come for a drink of water."

"Help yourself," said Fudu, and watched while Vundhla drank.

But Vundhla was in a mischievous mood, and decided to have some fun with Fudu. "Uncle," he teased, "those are funny little legs that you have. I am sure you couldn't run for any distance on them. Look at *my* beautiful long legs. None of the animals can catch me. When they *do* get a bit near, I just pop down a hole. Ha, ha, ha!"

"Look here, Vundhla, my legs suit me, and I can beat you in a race. Your long thin legs could not even carry my house – much less win a race!"

The hare rolled on the ground and squeaked with merriment, and when he had stopped laughing, suggested that they should have a race there and then.

"Uncle, we will run as far as that tall palm tree. It is only a hundred yards away. If you beat me, I will give you my favourite ox, which I value above all my cattle."

The tortoise thought the matter over, and gravely remarked, "When I run, Vundhla, I prefer miles, not yards. I will race you to Mushenje's Pan, which is only six miles away. You know the path, and we will start from here as the sun reaches noon. If *you* win, you can choose the best ox in MY herd. Let me see: today is Monday. We will run on Saturday. Now, go away, I want to sleep."

Vundhla agreed to the arrangement, and went home laughing.

Fudu wasted no time, and as soon as Vundhla was out of sight, he sent out bush messages to all his relations, telling each what he wanted him to do.

They were to place themselves at regular intervals along the path to Mushenje's Pan at noon on Saturday, (if possible just over a small rise) and were all to commence running immediately towards the Pan. They were to watch carefully and when Vundhla passed travelling at speed, they could go about their own business.

Fudu, having made them understand thoroughly the part they were to play, took a gourd with him, and started out for Mushenje's Pan. He arrived there on time on Saturday, filled his gourd with water, and set off along the path *towards* the starting point.

Vundhla arrived at the starting point also on time on Saturday, and so did Fudu's cousin. They shook hands, and the race began. Vundhla was out of sight in a few moments, and Fudu's cousin lost interest, though it was a long while before he could stop laughing.

Vundhla was laughing too, until he came to the top of the first little rise ahead, and saw tortoise No. 2 plodding along in front of him. He put on extra speed, and was soon out of sight, but he could not understand just how Fudu had managed it.

Another rise, and another. Each time Fudu was ahead, and laughed loudly as the hare passed him. Vundhla firmly believed, by this time, that the tortoise had learned to fly!

The sun was boiling hot, and Mushenje's Pan was still two miles away. Another rise, and STILL Fudu was ahead! Oh, why, he thought, did he leave Ramba Fountain, where the water was cool and sweet? His favourite ox seemed to be fading away!

He was drawing near to the Pan, however, so he put on his last spurt of speed. His breathing was heavy, and his throat was dry, when crash! he tripped and fell head over heels, and lay exhausted where he had fallen. He just could not go any further.

He fell asleep, with every limb trembling from the strain – but awakened again, and soon managed to get to his feet, and staggered on until he could see the winning post, with the stretch of cool water beyond.

But what was that? Someone was coming *towards* him carrying a gourd of water – and that "someone" was Fudu! This was more than he could stand, and he fainted.

Some time later Vundhla recovered, to find that he had been sprinkled with cool water, and felt a great deal better. He opened his eyes to see Fudu holding the gourd to his lips, and heard him saying in a soothing voice, "Take a drink of this, Son, I had an idea that you would be needing it!"

*

"You see," chuckled Chakuti, "Vundhla hadn't the brains to see just HOW he had been cheated!"

THE WHITE HORNBILL

Life was early astir on our camping days, and after a night beneath the stars, with God's clean air around us, we would rise with the dawn. On one particular morning we two children, fascinated as ever by the early, haunting boom of the big clumsy Ground Hornbill, borrowed Chakuti, and set off in great excitement to find the nest of a pair of these big birds, which he assured us was hidden in the roots of a wild fig tree over the hill. Growler, Farewell's beloved dog, of course chose to accompany us. He was ever our shadow.

The sun came up as we set out. A great orb of crimson, drenching the veld with soft sunshine. At that early hour one might meet anything. Creatures of the night, who had hunted far afield, were returning to their lairs. Those of the daylight and sunshine were stretching their limbs, and, like ourselves beginning a new day.

As it happened, it was a forager by night, whose path we crossed not long after we had left the camp.

Mrs. Nungu, the porcupine, with her two babies, was on her way home.

With a deep-throated bark of excitement, Growler was after them – before we had time to stop him. Porcupines are dangerous folk for a dog to meet.

We must have met Mrs. Nungu almost on her threshold for, with a great rattling of her hollow white tail-quills, she and her youngsters vanished down a large ant-bear hole.

Growler was on their heels, and we were too late to stop him from disappearing from view after them. He was too big a dog to go with safety down such a hole. One of the Irish Terriers from the farm would have fared better, being small enough to turn round when things got too hot for him. But Growler, digging as he pressed forward, merely blocked up the hole behind him, and his excited barking grew fainter and fainter, as the earth block grew thicker and thicker.

There was nothing, really, that we could do, except to sit nearby and hope that he would come out by one of the many exits that each porcupine warren contains.

It was very tantalising, for, from every direction seemed to come the "OOOP-OOOP-OOOP" of our elusive hornbills.

"How, Chakuti, can Singisi throw his voice like that?" asked Farewell, "for surely he must be over the hill?"

At one minute the call would seem to come from a few yards away, and yet there was no sign of his great black waddling figure, with the red goggles and wattles, whichever way we looked. The next moment the call would seem to come from miles away.

"We will wait until the hour for food has arrived," said Chakuti, "and, if your dog has not settled his account with 'the prickly one' by then, we will fetch a pick and a shovel to dig him out. He cannot make headway if the quills are against him."

We were greatly concerned for the safety of our pet – but we were more or less used to such happenings, and it would not have been the first time that a pick and shovel had released him.

We made a round of the many entrances and exits of the big warren, calling first down one hole, and then down another, to guide him by our voices, but without success.

The excited barking and digging had now ceased, and it seemed that there was nothing left to do, but to sit patiently, and hope that he would find his way out.

"Ooop-ooop-ooop," and then from seemingly a totally different direction, on a much lower note, the answering 'ooop-ooop-ooop."

There was a positive chorus all round us now, and we saw waddling into view five ridiculous ground hornbills.

"See," whispered Chakuti, "they are looking for their old enemy, the snake. The Big Lord was indeed good when He sent Singisi to rid us of the legless ones."

"Well we know, Chakuti, that you have a story to tell about Singisi; and seeing that we must await 'his lordship' down there, now is surely a good time to tell it! HOW does the big bird throw his voice?" asked Farewell, once more.

"It is a gift that has come from his big White Ancestor, who said that *always* when he called, no matter where he should be, yet should he be heard."

"Nonsense," we said, almost as one. "Whoever heard of a *white* Singisi? Black he is, and black he has been since the beginning of time."

"Not so, Children of the White Race. Time can still be counted since YOUR ancestors came to this land. How, then, can you speak of the things that happened here before even the big baobab trees took root upon the soil?*

"True enough, since that time, and for many generations before, no white Singisi has appeared. But it has been handed down that such was so.

"Listen, is that not your dog, that digs again?"

---

*The Africans say that as one never sees the beginning of the life of the baobab tree, i.e. a *tiny seedling*, they must have been there since the beginning of time.

By putting our ears to the ground, we could hear a faint scratching, and then silence once more.

We were well concealed behind the low bushes that surrounded the porcupine warren, so we had an excellent opportunity of watching the hornbill family as it waddled about in search of snakes and other dainties.

"See how quick Singisi is for all his clumsy walking," he whispered, as one of the hornbills darted at something, and, with an incredibly swift movement, threw it into the air, to pounce on and devour it as it touched the ground. "Our enemy the snake is dead before he knows what struck him. See the twist that breaks the neck! Surely, he IS the king of all snake-killers!"

"But is he better, then, than Dwai? (the Secretary bird). Always have I heard that *he* is the one for snakes?" I asked.

"Not so, Nkosizana; listen to the tale of Singisi.

You must know that in the young days of the world, the snake had no master. He was lord above the other creatures, for, because of his venom and of his wickedness none could stand against him.

The Bird People were great sufferers at his hand, and slowly were the snakes making a big slaughter in the bird lines. Not only did they suffer by the snakes' fondness for their eggs and their fledglings – but by the snake's power to make them helpless by the wickedness of his gaze.

A meeting of great urgency was called on the Big Plains, by the Feathered Ones, and it was decided to make a war on the snake tribe. They therefore banded themselves together in great bravery to attack the belly-walkers.

But, as you know, the advantage of the legless ones is great. Their poison-teeth and their speed are more than a match for any bird. True, the feathers take the first strength of the poison; while the bird can pursue from the air, to drop on the snake from above. But this is not enough.

So thus the war waged backwards and forwards, with the Snake People bringing great havoc to the Feathered Ones. Many were those who would not rise again.

A great victory for the snakes was close at hand when, from over the hills that bound the plain, came a battle challenge of great encouragement "ooop-ooop-ooop"; and then in a lower voice "OOOP-OOOP-OOOP", while into view there strode Singisi, with three of his kin.

The Snake People cowered, for well they knew the strength and speed of Singisi's beak.

First on this side, and then on that, did the great birds fling the Snake People, and each as he fell, lay limp and still, his neck all but severed.

A great hiss of fear arose from many divided tongues, and in answer, from out of the long grass, skimming o'er the waving tops, as though on wings, came to their aid the most deadly of them all; the dreaded Great Mamba.

With two lightning strokes he killed Singisi's brothers. He then hesitated, to consider his next move.

The mamba's wicked eyes glistened. He had only to await his time. Why hurry? He had Singisi and his wife at his mercy. He would wait a while until he was hungry; stale meat made an ill taste in the mouth.

"*Now* who is lord of all things?" he asked the birds. "NOW will I avenge my kind."

But courage dies hard in some. With snapping beak and blazing eye, Singisi turned to the Great Mamba and said:

"Why should the feathered Ones be beaten by YOU? You who have no legs and no wings. *You*, who crawl along the ground like a worm?"

Sometimes, White Children, when a big trouble comes to us, we lift up our eyes to the Spirits of our Ancestors, and call to them to help us. Thus did the defeated hornbill.

With only two of his kind left, he was in great distress – for surely now, the mamba in his pride, would kill him, and his wife too. Who, then would be left to carry on the fight?

He raised his great beak to the sky, and up to the Heavens went his far-reaching cry of "ooop-ooop-ooop" followed by the lower voice "OOOP-OOOP-OOOP!"

Almost as the last sound left his beak, there came a whirring of wings, and from the blue dome above him, there flew a pure white One of Their Kind, of great and dazzling beauty.

Straight at the mamba he flew, and with his sharp beak, he cut the snake into small pieces – and these pieces he scattered far and wide upon the length and breadth of the battlefield.

Thereupon he rose up again into the Heavens, as suddenly as he had come, and was seen no more.

Since that day, not even the deadly mamba has dared to face Singisi. Daily you will see him and his kind, seeking here, and seeking there. Ever is he on the search for the Snake People.

"And so, is not Singisi a great friend to Mankind?"

We were too busy digging Growler out of his trouble to continue our search for the hornbill's nest, and it was past noon on the following day before we rescued our sadder, but in no way wiser pet from what nearly was his grave.

It was a very sick dog that we found in the bowels of the earth, looking more like a pin-cushion than anything else.

We carried him with care back to the camp, where we removed the many quills that were embedded in him, and disinfected and bandaged his hurts.

Our holiday was at an end, so we made him as comfortable as we could on a soft bed in the wagon – and there he lay as we jolted over the rough road, back to the farm.

BATSWANA

Illustrated by
JILLIAN HULME

FOREWORD

In past years these traditional tales of my people have been passed down from parent to child and perpetuated. But as times change, and as education and forms of entertainment alter, these tales will become less and less known. Therefore, it is time that they were preserved in a written record, and I am delighted that Phyllis Savory has done so.

There is much beauty and interest in these tales, and I hope that people elsewhere will enjoy them as much as we in our country have done for many years.

SERETSE M. KHAMA

INTRODUCTION

Historians tell us that the White races first came into contact with the Bantu African at the beginning of 1500, although it was not until a great deal later that we came to know much about them. We are also led to believe that the Great Bantu Trek Southwards from Nyanzaland, the area to the North of Kenya and Uganda, began some 500 years earlier.

Without the ability to write, the Bantu People were obliged to rely upon the memories of their tribal historians to keep their history alive. It was the duty of these historians to learn the sequence of important happenings by heart. It was by the old grandparents (especially the old *women*) that the age-old Folk Fairy Tales were handed down from that time to the present day. Sometimes these old tales were told simply for the sake of amusement, to pass away the evening hours; but sometimes they were also expected to teach a moral, or to perpetuate an historical event.

These African Folk Tales follow very much the same pattern as do our European tales, telling of magic and ogres, fairy princes and talking animals, witches and wizards. Wherever there are people, the world over, there are tales: and from the Nyanzaland of long, long ago, originated the great network of Bantu Folk Tales that abound in Southern Africa today.

It can be readily understood, therefore, that from time to time these tales not only overlap, but telescope one into the other. Two interesting examples have been included in this book of tales belonging to some of the tribes who inhabit the area known today as Botswana.

This fact will be realised by those who have read some of the earlier "Fireside" tales, when they renew their acquaintance with Mmutla the hare, that "bad man of the wilds" who, in the Basuto version of this tale ties his thatching partner to the roof of the hut they are building, while in Kwa-Zulu it is the jackal who ties the lion to the roof, and so on. From Matabeleland the same rascally hare warns the lion (from whom he is trying to escape) to hold up the roof of the cave, and thus achieves his object. Again will be recognised, this time from Xhosaland, the woman who tested her husband's love too far, and came to grief in consequence.

These variations – and there are many of them – are to be found thousands of miles apart, to which diverse areas they have travelled by word of mouth over the period of the last 2 000 years, from the same homeland of Nyanza. This significant fact, and the deep interest of the particular tales, has decided me to re-tell them, this time following the variation belonging to the Batswana People.

As mentioned in earlier "Fireside" tales, the Zulu despot Chaka was the main comparatively recent cause of the wide-spread distribution of these age-old tales. Mzilikazi's flight from Chaka's anger in the early 1820's carried some of them to Bechuanaland through which country Mzilikazi blazed a trail on his way to conquer the present Matabeleland. In this manner his warriors picked up Batswana wives as they conquered, and left Zulu tales behind them.

In their trek from the North, the Batswana tribes travelled more or less down the centre of the continent of Africa and are, with the Vendas, known as the Highveld Bantu. The Nguni tribes of the Zulus, Xhosas and Fingoes, came down towards the East, and are known as the Lowveld Bantu, while the little yellow Bushmen kept to the West.

In the 222 000 square miles inhabited by the Batswana People, there are many kindred tribes. Among these are the Bamangwato, the Bangwaketse, the Batawana, the Bakwena, Bakgatla, Batlokwa, Bakalahari and the Barolong. I have been fortunate in obtaining the totem tales of some of these tribes, which add greatly to the interest of the collection.

To the best of my knowledge all the tales in this book are of pure Bantu origin, and although my readers might see a resemblance in "Ntabesana" to one of our own old nursery tales, this story is claimed by the Tswana People as their own. It is possible that it was told to his pupils by an early missionary, and has been both adopted and added to by these same pupils as they, in turn, have become grandparents. Such adaptations of our own old tales are to be met with in many parts of civilised Bantuland, and it is becoming increasingly difficult to separate them from those of pure Bantu origin.

1

THE STORY OF PUTI, THE DUIKER

A folk tale which was born in fact, and one which is very dear to the hearts of the people of the Bamangwato tribe of Botswana, concerns Puti, the little shy, grey and brown duiker with the white belly. The kindness of this little buck so moved Chief Khama I., the great-grand-father of Khama the Great, that he made it the totem, or emblem of his tribe*, instructing his subjects to venerate it for evermore.

In the days during which this came about, the Matabele warriors, under the leadership of the ruthless chief Mzilikazi, were ravaging and laying waste to vast areas of Botswana as they passed through the country, on their way to conquer the Mashona people who inhabited the area which was later to become Matabeleland, in the Zimbabwe of today.

As they passed through Chief Khama's homeland, the merciless hordes of Matabele swept all before them, and among their many victories had encircled the army of the Bamangwato tribe. Trapped when his warriors scattered, Khama had been forced to flee for his very life.

As may be imagined, a ruler of such importance would be a very valuable prize to capture, so the Matabele singled him out, straining every nerve and limb to take him, dead or alive, to their lord Mzilikazi. Each tried to outstrip his neighbour in the chase as gradually the "bloodhounds" wore their quarry down.

Closer and closer around him his enemies drew in the encircling net, but the chief was strong and planned, could he but escape alive, that he would rally his brave men so that they could fight again, and perhaps halt this oncoming "swarm of locusts" that was eating up his beloved land.

The chase wore on: Khama's breath came faster, and became more laboured; he stumbled from exhaustion – but the cry of joy that arose from his pursuers as they realised that his strength was failing, gave fresh impetus to the muscles of the weary man's legs and, wiping away the sweat that almost blinded him he struggled on.

*Originally the crocodile.

Ahead lay scattered bushland; he hoped that maybe he could reach it, and hide among the stunted shrubs, thus eluding his relentless hunters. But the chance was small indeed, for the warriors were drawing in upon him and keeping him constantly in view. He flogged his weary muscles into one last spurt of speed, and for a moment was lost to the sight of the merciless warriors who hunted him.

A tangled clump of thornbush lay close ahead of him. Could he reach it before they spotted him once more? His heart was pounding like the hoofbeats of a stampeding herd as he threw himself into its dense cover, worming his way among the shadows to the centre. The thorns tore at and impeded him as he eased himself behind a fallen log, and he was too distressed to realise that he was not the only fugitive that had sought shelter in its tangled fastness. Puti, the duiker was nestled beside the log – but the little creature did not move when the man brushed against him as he took refuge by his side.

Khama tried to quieten his thumping heart, and to hold his panting breath. "Be still, oh my heart," he prayed, "be still!"

Hard upon his heels came his relentless trackers. He heard them check their pace as they advanced. "We have him!" they cried excitedly, as they poked their assegais against the very log behind which he lay; "he cannot escape us now, for he is surrounded!"

Hardly had the word left their lips before out from the thicket in which he hid – from pressing against his very side, in fact – dashed the little duiker, Puti. Away through the line of warriors the little buck dodged, as though to draw them after him.

"Our quarry has escaped us after all!" the warriors exclaimed in crestfallen astonishment, as they lowered their spears. "Mpuzi* does not lie next to man. Had the one we seek been inside this thicket, our friend Mpuzi would have fled when *he* approached. Come, we waste our time. To the hunt!" and they hastened on, not thinking it worth their while to search the place from which the frightened duiker had fled.

The beloved chief of the Bamangwato people heaved a deep sigh of relief and gratitude. Surely the Great One had sent Puti to save him, or why had not such a timid little creature made his bid to escape when *he*, a dreaded human, had pressed so dangerously close to his fur-covered side?

*Matabele word for Duiker.

Khama himself had been too distracted at the time, to notice the soft little body that had rested so trustingly against his own.

*

This story has been told many times before – but can a story of such beauty be told too often? And can any reader wonder that the timid little duiker holds the love and affection of the people of the Bamangwato tribe?

Narrator: Miss Gaositive K. T. Chiepe.

2

TLODING PELA

Of the many rare and fabulous creatures that lived in the Africa of long, long ago, surely the most beautiful of them all was Tloding Pela, the rain-bird of the Bangwaketse tribe of Southern Botswana.

Although this bird was hailed as the harbinger of the eagerly awaited rains each year, Tloding Pela was also greatly feared, for he was as agressive as he was lovely to look upon. His body shone bronze and gold like the setting sun, with green intermingled. The strong, bold flight feathers, so greatly prized by young initiates on their approaching manhood, glinted with the unearthly green of the forbidding cloud that carries hail – while the chest, puffed with pride each time he alighted upon the Rakhunohunana river-pan*, put the sheen of the stately peacock to shame. He was beautiful beyond imagining.

Fierce, too, was Tloding Pela. So fierce, that only the very bravest among the youths dared hope to use his hard-won feathers as his proof of valour, thus entitling him to lead his mophato†. Few indeed dared even approach the haunts of this lovely bird, let alone pluck his feathers from him.

Therefore it was with feelings of sad foreboding that those who loved Mosimane, the dead chief's orphaned son, heard that the boy planned to win the coveted feathers from this rare bird.

"The time of my approaching manhood is close upon me," the boy replied sullenly, when his guardian uncle tried to impress upon him the perils that accompanied such an ambition, "and must I shame my sleeping ancestors by returning empty-handed; to be led, instead of *to lead* my fellow-fighters?"

"It is thus that the grey monkeys chatter – without thought or reason," his uncle reproved him. "Have you not learned that the season which brings Tloding Pela upon his yearly visit from his distant home is still many moons away? Modimo, The Hidden One, sends him only when our

---

*Depression of land, holding water in the dry season.
†Regimental age-group.

Thirstland is parched, and is ready to drink its allotted moisture from the skies above. How then, will you find him, when our land has only now begun the time of thirst?"

"The bidding of my heart must be obeyed," Mosimane replied stubbornly, "for the time to prove my worth approaches, and I would not fail: I go."

"But whither will you go, in this vast land?" asked the uncle, hoping to impress upon the boy the difficulty of the task of finding Tloding Pela. "None know the haunts of this fierce bird but those who deal in wizardry. At this parched season of the year, you would look for him in vain."

However, nothing that his uncle said would alter Mosimane's decision to search for the bird, and presently a feeling of pride in her nephew's determination arose within the bosom of his aunt, and she decided to help the boy whom she loved as her own. She therefore begged him to be patient, saying to those who tried to restrain him, "I will find the haunts of the dreaded Tloding Pela; the boy shall have his wish."

"What! A woman find the resting place of one of such fierceness, when brave men fail?" the villagers scoffed. But the aunt refused to listen to their taunts and, taking her magic lerumo*, and servants to drive ten fat oxen, she left to search for an old, old rain-doctor belonging to her tribe who, she knew, could help her if he would.

Day after day she travelled, following the trail of the old man as he went from one village to another; but it was a long, long time before she caught up with him. That this man could tell her where to find Tloding Pela she felt sure, for it was well known that portions of the bird's body-parts were used to strengthen the potency of his powerful rain medicines in times of drought.

The days having stretched into weeks, the woman had almost despaired of finding the man she sought, when she learned that he was but a short distance ahead, beyond a swiftly flowing river. Their hopes revived, the party hurried on to a gently sloping river bank ahead of them but, as the woman approached the water's edge, a string of bubbles rose to the surface and the water parted to show the head of a fearsome water-beast.

There was a gasp of terror from the attendants behind her, but the aunt bravely refused to let the creature bar her path. Backwards she

*Spear.

slowly moved towards her companions, and as she moved, so she sang to it and, charmed by the sweetness of her voice, the big beast followed.

Farther and farther away from its water home the woman moved until, reaching the safety of the firmer ground she stood and waited.

Soon it reached her side, and as it prepared to seize her in its jaws, she plunged the magic spear deep into the monster's chest. But a woman's thrust is weak, and she failed to pierce the leathery heart. Blood flowed freely from the gaping wound and the water tinged with crimson as, at the following stab, the creature slithered back into its watery home and died – and there she left it.

At last the river was crossed, and the party found the man they sought. "Daughter," he said, when she had made known to him the reason for her visit, "you ask me to divulge to you the alighting-place of Tloding Pela – but my price is high, for between the bird and me is a bond of secrecy. As all men know, I use portions of his body parts to make my potent brews, whereby to call down the life-giving rain from the sometimes cloudless skies. For this important rite I must obtain my ingredients by stealth and guile, so that their strength may aid me in my art. What have you to offer in return, should I tell you what you ask?"

"I have brought ten fat oxen, oh Great One," she replied. "The best in my husband's herd. All these are yours, for my need is great."

"It is well," said the old man, trying to hide the glint of satisfaction in his eyes, "I will tell you. Unless I bring him by my magic, the bird will not come again for many moons, but I will call him – for I see that your heart is true. Listen to me with care. Where the river Rakhunohunyana runs between Losabanyana and his smaller brother-hill, is a vast expanse of water-land. It is upon this place that Tloding Pela alights to carry out his duties to the Rain Queen. But remember, *you approach him at your peril!* I have finished." And, taking no further notice of the woman, the old rain-doctor gazed past her into the distance as though she was as the air about him. Maybe his thoughts were upon the fine addition to his precious herd – or maybe upon deeper matters. It mattered not to the woman, for she had gained the knowledge that she sought.

Now at last she could assist her beloved nephew to carry out his ambition, and for this her heart was glad. Her magic spear would surely protect him in his combat with the bird, so she sped home upon joyful feet.

Soon after her return, Mosimane, armed with his aunt's magic lerumo and a strong ox-hide shield, departed upon his quest. He encountered great hardships upon the way, and on many days he hungered, for fellow-beings were few and far between. On some days it was a handful of roots dug up by the wayside, that eased his empty stomach, and on others his spear brought down a hare if he was fortunate enough to see one – but eventually he reached his goal.

Tall green reeds and luscious grass fringed the pan that greeted his eager eyes at last, and the country round about was good to look upon for it was early autumn, when the rains had already left the land, and the earth was smiling from the results of her life-giving moisture.

But of Tloding Pela there was not a sign, so Mosimane settled down in the tall reeds to watch and wait. To the young, time means but little, and many days had passed before a loud whirring broke upon the stillness of the peaceful countryside. Then, with the speed of an arrow released from a bow, the bird streaked from beyond the boy's furthest vision, to alight with the grace of a dancer upon the tranquil water.

The old rain-doctor had kept his word to Mosimane's aunt and, with the arrival of the bird, the unexpected happened. The heavens opened, and the rain teemed down from a cloudless sky, at a time when no rain was due – for Tloding Pela had been summoned, and the roll of thunder that followed his arrival was enough to split the heavens.

The storm ended as quickly as it had begun, and once more the countryside was bathed in sunshine. Slowly the crest of the fierce bird rose as he sensed an unseen danger, and his sharp eyes searched the horizon for the foe he felt was awaiting him – and all this while Mosimane's thumb tested the sharpness of his aunt's magic spear. Then, using all the veld-craft that he knew, the youth crept from his place of hiding.

Edging his way through the reeds towards his quarry, the boy was within throwing distance before it saw him and, as the bird raised its wings and bore down upon him, Mosimane threw his aunt's magic spear.

Sometimes, however, over-keenness is apt to spoil the trueness of the eye, and the boy's heart missed a beat as he watched his trusted weapon flash harmlessly past its target, to be lost to sight in the depths of the swamp beyond. Only the ox-hide shield now remained to protect Mosimane against the fierce bird's anger, and he called loudly upon the spirits of his ancestors to aid him, as the creature advanced to the attack.

First one gained the advantage, and now the other, as backwards and forwards the fight raged. The bird's great speed was in his favour and the powerful beak struck viciously at the unprotected parts of Mosimane's body as he dodged from side to side to escape the punishing blows. But the boy's shield-work was also swift, and in the end the sharpness of his wits proved a match for the bird's beak. He finally brought an end to the fight when, snatching a handful of Tloding Pela's strong green wing-feathers, he fell upon the ground with the shield completely covering him and there, like an enormous tortoise he lay.

As soon as the bird had recovered from its surprise, a bitter tug-of-war began, as it pulled to free itself from Mosimane's relentless grasp until, one by one, the feathers pulled free from Tloding Pela's tired wing, and the bird fell exhausted to the ground. The boy had won his prize!

Again the thunder pealed and lightning flashed, while Mosimane heard heavy raindrops drumming upon the shield that covered him. When the storm had ceased, he carefully raised the shield and looked around him. Of Tloding Pela there was not a sign, and only the handful of feathers was left as proof of the victory that he had gained.

His distress at the loss of his aunt's magic spear was compensated by the outcome of his quest and, rejoicing, the youth went home. It was with pride that he thrust the precious proof of his success into his uncle's hand, to be held in trust for him until he had passed his manhood's tests.

There was little to fear in the hardships ahead, to one who had braved and overcome the dreaded Tloding Pela; Mosimane stood his trials with fortitude and distinction. And when finally the great day arrived on which the testing of the youths was completed, it was a joyful uncle who held aloft the coveted bunch of this bird's brilliant feathers, as he summoned all the headmen of the kingdom to a kgotla* to witness the boy's enrolment as the rightful leader of his regimental age-group. And it was a proud youth, too, who was presented to his companions that day.

In due course the chieftainship of his dead father was awarded to Mosimane, and he ruled his people well and wisely until the end of his days. His name still lives throughout the land that knew him, in that of *Tlodi-jamosimane*, as this pan is called even to this day.

Narrator: Mokabathebe K. Monnamme. 60 years of age.

*Meeting.

3

THE DISCOVERY OF FIRE

The people of Botswana will tell you that when man first came to live upon the earth, he was unaware of the existence of fire. His foods were the natural products of Mother Earth, placed upon it by the good Modimo – "The Hidden One". Bulbs, roots and fruit were plentiful in the countryside around him, and he ate the raw flesh of the game that abounded in the land. From the soft-eyed cows, which were Modimo's greatest gift of all, came health-giving milk, which was the daily drink of both young and old alike.

There was little to trouble him in the way of clothing, for the weather was mild, and the rays of the sun caressed his naked body as he basked in its warmth by day, whilst at night-time the softly braided skins of wild animals provided all the protection that was required against the winter cold. Man was fortunate indeed, and life was good.

Of fire he had neither need nor knowledge, and therefore he did not miss it. But it came about that on a certain cold and cloudy day, a man picked up his spear, and went to search for food. Far, far from home he travelled; beyond all the landmarks that he knew. Eventually a strange stillness caused him to pause and listen. There was a deep silence too, so his eyes scanned the countryside ahead until he saw a tall, thin cloud lazily spiralling up to the heavens.

"This is strange," he muttered to himself. "Never before have I seen a cloud drift upwards in this shape and manner, for it is surely climbing from the very earth itself. I must investigate!"

He approached the place with awe, and the nearer he drew to the rising cloud, the more intrigued he became until he found, on the threshold of a cave-like excavation, a fire burning cheerfully – while from it up to the sky, there rose, upon the still air, a long thin wisp of smoke.

Good manners were natural to the man, so he greeted the fire civilly. "Good-day to you, stranger," he said. "I have lived in this land since ever I drew breath, yet I have neither seen nor heard of your kind before. Tell me, to whom do I speak?"

"I return your greeting, Two-Legged-One," replied the fire pleasantly.

"I am one of the good Modimo's many servants. Come nearer, for the day is cold: you are welcome to thaw your hands in the warmth of my smile."

The man approached the fire, and his cold body was at once comforted by the warmth that enveloped the side of him that was nearest to the blaze. He sat down upon his haunches to enjoy for a while the strange creature's friendly hospitality, and the two chatted, each of the matters nearest to his heart. The warmer the man became, the happier and more contented he felt, until he thought how pleasant it would be to have this new friend visit *his* home, so that his wife and children could experience the wonderful feeling of well-being that radiated from his unusual companion and, maybe, he could even keep him in his home forever!

For this reason, therefore, before the man took his leave, he invited the fire to return the compliment by paying a visit to *his* home, where he could promise him a warm welcome not only from himself, but from his wife and children too. But to his great disappointment the fire declined the invitation, although assuring the man of his *own* welcome upon future visits.

The man returned to his home delighted with his adventure, and at once related to his family all that had befallen him. "He was beautiful beyond words," the husband told his wife. "He wore a red and yellow wrap about himself; and as his laughter crackled, many little stars drifted upwards from the ever-changing shape that is his mouth. But, my wife, you should have seen his breath! It gathered as a cloud above him – and when a gentle breeze wafted it towards me, a violent fit of coughing shook me. And how he laughed at this!"

"Husband, I am filled with a great curiosity to see this friendly being. Can you not bring him to visit us?"

The man told his wife of the fire's disinclination to leave his home, but promised to try again. This he did, not only once, but on many occasions that followed when he returned to further his friendship with the strange creature. But whenever he approached his host with the request to visit his wife and children, the fire excused himself upon one pretext or another.

Each time that the husband returned from these visits, he had fresh wonders to relate about the fire, until both his wife and children begged so earnestly to see his wonderful friend, that the man approached him with tears as he told of his wife's pleadings. "Why," he asked, "do you refuse my request to give you hospitality? Am I not your friend?"

"*Indeed* you are my friend," the fire assured him, "and it hurts me to refuse your wish. You must be patient with me if I seem to be ungracious; the truth is, I am afraid to leave my home for, whenever I do, a trail of destruction follows me."

"That would be as nothing, compared to the joy that your presence would give to my wife and children," the man assured him. Therefore, after many further refusals, an appointment was made one day, and the man was so overjoyed that he ran the whole way back to his home to give his wife the good news.

Excitement mounted high in the man's home when the great day arrived, and a sumptuous feast was prepared for their honoured guest. Everything was ready *hours* before the appointed time.

The fire left his cave in a quiet, orderly manner. But as he progressed along the path that had been worn between his home and that of his human friend, his fingers snatched at the dry grass upon either side, feeding it into his ever-ready mouth. And as he grew in stature, so also he grew in fierceness.

From the grass along the wayside, the snatching hands soon grasped the bushes upon which to feed the now voracious mouth. Bushes were soon too small; trees came next. And as the conflagration grew, so behind him rose the wind to speed the demon of destruction upon his way, until the whole countryside was ablaze.

From his distant home the man and his family glimpsed the fire's quiet departure from his dwelling, as a plume of smoke rose up into the sky. "My friend comes!" cried the man excitedly. "See, that is his breath, of which I told you. Soon you will see him in all his beauty. Look, he dances as he comes, for he is happy to be visiting us!"

Before long, small tongues of flame could be seen reaching upwards. "Yes, beautiful indeed," exclaimed his wife and children together, although a trifle uncertainly. "We are indeed honoured that he should come to see us."

It certainly was a lovely sight, made slightly awesome by the enormous columns of billowing smoke that now reached up to the very heavens. But presently birds began to fly past in terror, trying to escape the pursuing flames, and buck with heaving sides fled from the scorching heat; all trying to escape from the monster which they could not understand. The man's precious cows lowed in distress as they, too, with their calves at heel, fled for their lives. Soon a distant, wicked, crackling laugh was heard – though it was quickly drowned in a mighty roar as the fire bore down upon them.

"Husband," faltered the now terrified woman, as the childrens' eyes grew round in wonder, "are you *sure* that your friend means us no harm? We are afraid of him!"

"Woman," answered her husband uncertainly, "I, too, am afraid, for I have never seen him in this mood before. I will reason with him, and plead with him to come more gently." And loudly the man cried out to the advancing conflagration, beseeching him either to return to his home, or failing that, to come more quietly. But the fire turned a deaf ear to his pleadings: the flames grew wilder and yet wilder, until at last they had consumed everything in their path.

The man and his family now also took to their heels, following the frightened creatures that had fled before them. But as they ran, so the fire gained upon them until, worn out and breathless, they reached a broad and shallow river-crossing. Into the water they splashed, to cool their heated bodies, which were already scorched by the hot breath of their relentless pursuer.

The cool, calm water revived them – but they hurried on until, looking fearfully over his shoulder, the man saw to his surprise that the fire was no longer following them. "What miracle is this?" he panted as he tried to comfort the sobbing child he carried. "The water has saved us. The one whom I looked upon as my friend, is afraid to follow. See, our precious cattle are safe upon the bank beyond. We are saved!" and, scrambling onto the dry ground, the husband, wife and children threw themselves upon the grass and wept for joy.

The fire died out slowly as it reached the water's edge, although well into the night the man watched the blazing tree-trunks lighting up the forest across the water and, when morning came, he went to look at the place where his home had been. An ugly, charred and blackened waste greeted him for as far as his eye could see and, inside the skeleton of poles that had been his hut, he found the remains of the feast that had been prepared for their honoured guest.

The man picked up one of the burnt roots, and the delicious odour that came from it caused him to put it into his mouth. "Wife!" he exclaimed excitedly, "The feast that awaited our guest has not been spoiled – it has been improved! Come, we will eat it, for there is naught else left in this blackened desolation with which to satisfy our hunger. But," he added, "never, never again will I ask that demon of destruction to visit our home!"

Thus it was that after man had learned to *tame* fire, and to use the warmth of its flames for his bodily comfort, he also learned to improve his food by cooking it. First he roasted the roots and vegetables that grew throughout the countryside, and then he cooked the raw flesh of the animals he hunted – until today Fire is one of "The Hidden One's" most valued gifts to Man.

Narrator: Miss Goasitive K. T. Chiepe.

4

THE BOY NTABESANA

In a small pretty village on the edge of a gloomy forest in Botswana, there lived a little Tswana boy named Ntabesana, with his father, mother, brothers and sisters. It was a happy life for the children, but one of anxiety for the parents because, beyond the forest which was near at hand, there lived a wicked dimo*, whose favourite food was the tender flesh of little children. From time to time the people in the village suffered from this creature's raids until, one day, their chief decided to move his village into an area of open country some miles away, where precautions could be taken against the visits of their troublesome enemy.

When Ntabesana heard that he was to leave his beloved forest home, he begged to be allowed to remain behind, assuring his parents that to leave it would break his heart. "Leave me, mother," he begged, "for the love of my forest home is in my heart: take me from it, and I will die!"

"No, my child," his mother warned him, "if we leave you here alone, the wicked dimo will surely eat you."

His parents argued with the boy to no avail, until finally they agreed upon a plan. He could continue to live in his old home until they had built a new one on the far-away plainlands, in its exact likeness. "But," his mother added, "you must promise to keep yourself securely fastened in the safety of the hut. I will bring food to you from day to day, and when I reach the hut I will sing – and you know my voice – 'Ntabesana, Ntabesana, this is your mother, bringing your food!' Should, however, the dimo catch you by his wiles, you must be sure to fill your hands with ashes, and leave a trail for me to follow."

While the big exodus from the village took place, the dimo watched from the shelter of the forest, and as the last of the people disappeared from sight over the horizon he walked boldly through the deserted homes. Through all, that is to say, except one, and to this one he could not gain admittance. "Ah!" he muttered to himself, "It is fastened from the *inside*. Someone must be hiding in it. I will watch from the cover of the forest,

*Cannibal.

for maybe there is a dinner awaiting me within!" So, concealing himself among the trees, he kept the hut in view.

For two days he never left his place of hiding, and upon each day he saw Ntabesana's mother go to the hut with food for the child. He watched as she knocked upon the door, and he heard her sing as she did so, "Ntabesana, Ntabesana, this is your mother, bringing your food." He noted that the door was immediately unfastened and, after the food had been handed to the boy, he watched as the mother embraced her child.

"Ah!" smiled the dimo, "This should be easy. I will sing likewise and the child, thinking that I am his mother, will open the door to me!" Therefore, shortly before noon on the following day the dimo knocked upon the door, singing as he did so, "Ntabesana, Ntabesana, this is your mother, bringing your food." But he had forgotten the gruffness of his voice, and the child answered, "Go away, dimo. I know that it is you, by the gruffness of your voice. My mother's voice is soft and gentle. Go away!"

The cannibal went away disappointed, wondering what he could do to soften his harsh voice. "Perhaps," he thought, "if I burnt my throat, I would speak more softly." So he heated a stone in the fire intending to swallow it – but it burnt his tongue so badly that it did not get as far as his throat.

"Perhaps if I sing in a *low* voice," he thought, "the child will think it is his mother." So he lowered his voice on the following day, although it still remained malevolent.

But the child was not to be taken in this time either. "*Go away dimo*," he shouted through the door. "Your voice is low, but is also harsh. My mother's voice is low, but it is gentle – which yours could *never* be." Again the dimo had to admit defeat.

He wandered back to the forest through the deserted homes, and as he passed the village lime-pit, he took a handful of coarse lime and swallowed it. Ah! It rasped as it went down. He spoke, and his voice was hoarse and low, as though he had a cold – so he returned to the boy's hut and began to sing outside the door. He was surprised and delighted to hear how gentle his tone had become, and this time it *did* deceive Ntabesana, who opened the door to him.

Too late the boy realised his mistake but, remembering the last instructions given by his mother, he rushed to the back of the hut as the giant came inside the door and, while he was hastily filling his hands with ash, the dimo caught and put him into a big skin bag. Once inside the bag, Ntabesana made a small hole in the bottom, and through this he sprinkled the ash along the path as the dimo carried him towards the home where he lived, intending to cook the child for dinner for his wife and himself.

On the way their path passed near to a village at which a dance was in progress, and from which laughter and singing floated to them on the evening breeze. "No one will notice if I join the fun," said the giant to himself. "I could do with some refreshment, for my load is heavy, and it is long since I have eaten." So, going into the village he propped the bag against the wall of one of the huts and mingled with the crowd.

Presently a party of children playing outside saw the bag and, being full of curiosity as all children are, one of them kicked it. "Wow!" cried a voice from within it, "Your toes are sharp: you hurt me!"

"Did you hear?" the children whispered one to the other. "A human voice! Let us look inside." So they untied the string that fastened the bag and, on hearing Ntabesana's tale they hid him in a hut, putting a dog in his place in the bag.

It was not long before the dimo became tired of the fun and, picking up his bag slung it over his shoulder again, to continue upon his way towards the home where his wife awaited the arrival of her dinner.

After travelling for some distance the dog became restless and began to struggle. "Be still, or I will give you something for which to struggle!" threatened the dimo. The dog, however, continued its efforts to get out of the bag, and ended by biting the dimo's back through it.

"Eh! So you would use your teeth, would you?" thundered the dimo as he quickened his pace. "Wife," he called approaching his hut, "mmama-palo!"*

Reaching the doorway, he found that the fire was already blazing merrily so, without waiting to tip his load out onto the floor, he flung the bag straight onto the flames. There was a yelp of pain after it had burst open, and the dog, scrambling out of the fire, rushed through the open door, to disappear into the distance.

The dimo was both surprised and angry. Especially so when the woman turned to scold him saying, "Is *this* the joke you play upon a starving wife? Find some food for me at once, or I will leave you."

*Light the fire.

The dimo hastened back to Ntabesana's forest home, hoping that the boy had found his way back to it. But the door was unfastened, and all that he found was the trail of ash scattered along the pathway. He followed the trail, rubbing out all traces of it with his foot as he went, until finally reaching the hut against which he had rested the bag while he joined in the village fun.

He found the place completely deserted and, as there was not a soul in sight, was forced to return empty-handed to his angry wife. "*Fetch me some human flesh!*" was the only reply he got when he told her of his fruitless search. So he went away again and for many days endeavoured to fulfil his wife's demand, but not a stray nor an unprotected child could he find. In the end, when he finally returned downhearted and empty-handed to his home, he realised that his wife had carried out her threat and had left him, for the place was completely deserted.

Ntabesana continued to live in the village of his rescuers for, the ash having been obliterated by the dimo, he could not find his way back to his old home on the edge of the forest. Neither could his mother find her son, for the very same reason; and when the sorrowing woman told her chief of the boy's disappearance, he scolded her for her disobedience in leaving him behind. "The fault is yours alone," he said, "you did not obey my orders!" and with this poor comfort, Ntabesana's mother had to be satisfied.

Narrator: Botsile Molokela.

5

TSWANA

Tswana, like all spoiled and pampered young people the world over, was not only a wayward youth – he was a very disobedient one as well. He was now eighteen years old, by which time he should have settled down to the normal occupations and duties of his age-group companions; however, from his earliest childhood his parents had encouraged him in idleness, allowing him to indulge his every wish. Finally he became so unruly that his father could bear with his laziness no longer, and thrashed him soundly.

Instead of regretting his waywardness, and accepting his punishment as an obedient and docile son should, Tswana felt nothing but anger at his father's punishment and, without waiting to collect even provisions for his journey, he ran away.

From village to village the boy wandered, begging food and shelter upon the way. Mile after mile he trudged, giving no thought to his future plans until, unfortunately treading upon a thorn one day, his foot became poisoned and very painful indeed.

"Eh!" he sighed, as he hobbled towards a rise ahead of him, "Would that I could find some food and shelter, for I can walk no farther. The wind surely is as sharp as the thorn that pricked me! How grateful would I be for a good hot meal to warm me."

The words had scarcely passed his lips before, on reaching the crest of the rise, he saw a light flickering spasmodically in the distance. He hastened his painful, flagging footsteps towards it, and soon limped up to a small clearing beside a spreading tree. In the neatly kept little clearing in front of it was the very tallest man whom he had ever seen; it seemed to Tswana that this giant's head reached to the tops of the very trees themselves, and he was as thin as he was tall. By the side of the fire sat a sad-faced girl, silently poking the embers of a dying fire back to life.

"Dumela rra; dumela mma*, he said to them.

The tall man and his companion returned his greetings, after which the

---

*Good-day sir; good-day madam.

man motioned him to sit down and join them at the meal that they were about to begin. With a sigh of relief and weariness, Tswana sat down and did full justice to all that was put before him.

"You are tired, my friend," sympathised the tall man. "You must rest here for the night, and tomorrow my daughter and I will speed you upon your journey, to wherever it may lead you. In the meantime, before I take my usual evening stroll abroad, I will wish you good-night." And he vanished into the fast falling evening shadows.

"Alas, alas!" cried the girl as soon as the giant was beyond hearing, "What ill-fortune has brought you to this dreadful place? My father is a cruel cannibal who has already eaten his own father, mother, wife and son – and what is more, he has forced me to join him in his human feasts. You must leave at once, for tomorrow he will make a meal of *you!*"

But Tswana's foot was so swollen and painful by now, that he could not put it to the ground, let alone run upon it, and he realised that the giant's mighty steps would soon out-strip even the fastest runner. "I cannot leave tonight," he replied miserably; "I must remain here and accept my fate."

However, the giant's daughter comforted him by suggesting that, as her father had eaten well that day, she did not think he need fear for his safety until the *following* day. But in spite of her words of comfort, Tswana spent a worried and a wakeful night.

Strange as it is to say, although the giant was so very much taller than many of his victims, he was able to overcome them only when they took their eyes off him, so that his killings had therefore to be brought about by guile. On this account he lost no time in preparing a plot whereby to trick Tswana, and it was for this reason that he asked him upon the following morning if he could play the six-stringed Bakwena guitar which hung in his hut? Tswana was surprised at such a question but, thinking that perhaps his host was genuinely fond of music, and also wishing to humour the creature, he admitted that he could.

"Visitors so seldom come this way," explained the giant, "that your arrival calls for an *especial* celebration. Come, let us be merry! You shall play the music, while I shall dance for you." He went to his hut to fetch the guitar, and while he was away his daughter whispered to Tswana, "Do not trust him; and if you wish to get the better of him, do not take your eyes from him – even for an instant."

When the giant returned, it was not only his guitar that he brought from his hut; he also carried in his hand a freshly sharpened battle-axe.

"Of what use can such a weapon be, when you wish to celebrate with song and dance?" Tswana asked him suspiciously.

"Ah!" lied the giant with cunning, "I am noted far and wide for the skilful manner in which I execute the 'Battle Dance', and I thought that it might interest you to watch me dance it. *Come*, strike up some catchy folk tunes first; we will leave the best dance until the last." Of course the wicked creature intended that Tswana should become so intent upon his playing that he would bend his head over the guitar and, thus baring his neck, provide an opportunity to strike the fatal blow. And thus the dance began.

During all this time Tswana's eyes never ceased to follow the dancer's every movement, and not even for one instant did he take them off the swiftly moving figure – while the woman sat silently watching the pair of them.

The giant at last began to tire: the lad was proving too smart for him. He must end this farce, he decided. "Now for the Battle Dance," he called out, snatching at the axe as he passed the spot where he had previously laid it upon the ground, and Tswana, his eyes still fixed upon the giant's every movement, at once struck up the wild notes.

Backwards and forwards leapt and sprang the tall, agile figure, awaiting his opportunity. Closer and closer he swung the sharp-edged battle-axe; now feinting, now as though he dodged some awesome foe although, with the youth's eyes so keenly fixed upon him, he never found a chance to strike the blow that would decapitate his intended victim.

"Of a truth, the youngster is too clever for me!" thought the giant, and his breath came faster as his pace increased – but never once did Tswana give him the opportunity that he sought – "He is as wily as Phokoye the Jackal," he muttered to himself. "I must seek elsewhere for my meal today, for I can dance no longer. I will catch him unawares tomorrow."

"Stranger," he addressed the boy as he came to a halt, "you play as one possessed, but my bones are not as young as they were in the past. Tomorrow *I* will call the tune, and *you* will dance to it."

"When my foot is less painful," replied Tswana, "I will show you such dancing as you have never seen before!" and with this promise the giant had to be satisfied.

Cheated out of his human feast, the giant was forced to hunt his food for the following day, and he went out after they had eaten, a disappointed and a disgruntled man. "You must flee *at once*," the daughter warned Tswana as soon as her father was out of sight. "You must not stay here for another hour."

"But *still* I cannot," replied the youth despondently, holding up his foot for her to see. "My foot will not allow me even to put it to the ground – so how could I flee? Your father would overtake me with ease."

"Then I will help you yet again," promised the girl, "although by doing so I must seal my fate. In two containers my father keeps his magic medicines. From one of these he will give you a potion to drink tonight before you go to sleep, for you have been too clever for him today. He will tell you that it is a draught to keep the mosquitoes from biting you, but in reality it is a powerful drug which will make you lose consciousness and thus, while you are at his mercy, he will kill you.

"The other mixture is a balm which gives vitality and strength. This is the medicine he takes himself, that he may be strengthened to enable him to eat you at one sitting. I will change the places of the medicines, so that *he* will be the one to lose conciousness, while *you* will be endowed with added vigour to enable you to escape in safety.

True to her promise, the daughter put the wrong container into her father's hand when he called for the mosquito mixture, and he watched with gloating eyes as their "honoured guest" drained it to the dregs. Then he himself, gulped down the contents of the second pot – and it was not long before a feeling of great drowsiness began gradually to overcome him and he lapsed into a deep, deep sleep.

For three full days the giant lay thus incapacitated, while the strengthening medicine sped the boy Tswana onwards to his father's home. But it is not every tale that has a happy ending, and this one ends in sadness because, although Tswana lived for many years in the bosom of his family, not even the careful and devoted nursing of his sorrowing mother was able to cure his poisoned foot, and it never healed. Thus Tswana carried the result of his quarrel with his father to the grave with him.

His wayward childhood, too, brought trouble upon the girl whose bravery had saved him in his need because, when finally her father awakened from his long sleep, to realise the trick that she had played upon him, he was so angry that he sent her to join her grandmother, grandfather, mother and her brother!

This story goes to prove that to spoil a child in his early years, is to reap trouble for him in later life, and to bring sorrow to those who love him. It is a warning both to children and to their parents.

6

THE POWER OF TAWANA*

For many years a Batawana man and wife had longed to hear childish laughter brighten the solitude of their lonely hut; but throughout their married life their wish had remained unfulfilled, leaving them sad of heart. When, therefore, the woman told her husband that this longstanding wish would at last be gratified, he said to her, "Woman, during all the years that we have been man and wife, I have loved you dearly – but from this time onward that love will be doubled. And upon the day on which you put a man-child into my arms, I will grant your greatest wish, no matter what it might be."

The months passed, and in the course of time a son was born to them, so that their happiness should have been complete. But a threatening cloud of doubt crept into the woman's mind, and she planned that she would *test* the love that her husband had declared to her.

"Husband," she said, "I have given you your man-child, and now I would remind you of the promise that you made to me. I request that you bring to me the liver of a lion, that I may eat it."

Hearing this, the man was sore afraid and he replied, "Where shall I get it, my wife?"

The woman pouted her lips as she said, "Then your promise was as nothing, my husband. You do not love me after all!"

The husband was deeply hurt and greatly distressed at his wife's cruel words and he decided that, cost him what it might, he would grant her wish. For many days he remained silent, as he brooded on a plan.

"Guile alone will enable me to obtain the liver of the mighty lion," he decided. "But how should I set about it?"

Just then he caught sight of a lion skin that hung across the rafters of his hut, and an idea began to form in his mind. "I will use this skin," he thought, "to disguise myself. And as I cannot hope to match myself against a full-grown beast, I must be satisfied with a cub – for my wife did not mention *size*."

*The lion cub.

He laid his plans carefully and, on the following day, without saying anything to his wife, took the skin, and some ditloo nuts* to eat upon the journey and left for a nearby forest, in which he knew there lived a pride of lions.

For a long while he searched in vain, until at last he saw them sleeping in the shade of a large spreading thorn tree. He threw a small stone into their midst to test their wakefulness, but they never stirred. "Ah, I am fortunate indeed, for they have eaten heavily," he thought, as he covered himself with the lion's skin.

With the utmost care, using some gut and a long thorn that he had brought with him, he sewed himself into the softly-braided lion skin. When this was done to his satisfaction, he quietly crept among the sleeping lions and, lying down, pretended that he was one of them.

Later, when their rest had been completed, the lions awoke and jumped suddenly to their feet, for they sensed a strange presence in their midst. The man did his best to imitate them, but his actions were clumsy. "This is not a lion; it is a human," said one of the creatures suspiciously.

The lion sniffed the stranger, but the smell was of his own kind, so he

*Small ground-nut.

hesitated. At that moment another lion interrupted him saying, "Come, we will test him. Let us eat stones, for it is well known that humans cannot crunch stones as *we* can. If he is a human, he will betray himself soon enough."

But the man was too clever for them, and when they began to crunch the stones, he threw down the ditloo nuts and crunched those. The lions were satisfied, and accepted him as one of themselves.

The afternoon wore on and the lions, still replete from their earlier kill lazed under the big tree, taking no further notice of the stranger until finally, as the dark closed in around them, they slept.

On the following morning his companions rose early and prepared for their daily hunt. "I am sick," said the man, "I cannot hunt today. And as I would be of no assistance to you in the chase, I shall remain with the children."

Again the suspicious one grumbled, "He is a man, I tell you!" But his companions scoffed at his warning and said, "He is a lion. Let us go."

The man remained behind and, no sooner were the lions out of hearing, then he quickly killed one of the cubs. Taking the liver, he left the flesh untouched, and departed for his home in haste.

"See, my wife," he said upon arrival, "I have fulfilled your wish." And he threw down at her feet, the liver of the lion cub.

The woman greeted her husband with pleasure, and at once cooked and ate the liver with relish. But no sooner had she done so, than her throat became dry and parched, burning with such fierceness that she thought she would die.

She called for water, which her husband brought to her – but the more she drank, the more thirsty she became until in despair, she went to consult Phiri the hyena, who was a well-known witch-doctor of the wilds.

"You need water from a very still pool," he said, "A pool in which Segogwane the frog has never been." It was night time by then, and the hyena raised his hideous voice to the full moon in a raucous sound that was suspiciously like a laugh.

The woman's thirst was so agonizing that she did not wait until the morning, but left at once upon her search. From stream to stream she went; but in each as she neared it, she heard in Segogwane's voice a mocking croak – as on and on she trudged.

She was near to collapsing from thirst and fatigue when she came at last to a clear, still pool, in which no frog had ever been. It was, in fact the animals' drinking pool. Sinking down to the ground with a sigh of relief the woman drank, and drank, and *drank*, until her stomach became so distended that she was unable to rise from the ground. She was astonished to see that she had drunk the pool completely dry; there was not a drop of water left.

Here the woman was forced by the weight of her stomach, to sit until shortly after midday, when Mmutla the hare came to quench his thirst. Seeing the empty pool he asked, "Where is our water?"

"My big stomach drank it," replied the woman.

Mmutla pondered the matter for a while, but no solution occurred to him, so he thumped his hind-feet upon the ground to show his displeasure, and went upon his way.

The next animal to appear upon the scene was Tlou the elephant: fortunately he was not very thirsty so, after the woman had given the same reply to his question about the water, he went upon *his* way without making a fuss.

Thakadu the ant-bear, however, badly needed a drink after his meal of peppery ants – he was very thirsty indeed – but as there was nothing that *he* could do about it, he ambled off into the long grass grumbling and disgruntled.

Khudu the tortoise had taken several days to get to the waterhole from the dry area in which he lived, as his legs were very short. He was very disappointed, because although a tortoise can live for long periods without water, he enjoys a drink from time to time. He turned away without a word, in the hope of finding some succulent leaves upon which to quench his thirst.

Kgabo the monkey was really only passing by, but being an inquisitive little creature, thought that he would just drop in at the animals' usual meeting place, to learn the gossip of the forest, for it had come to his ears that the woman had seen a mythical creature of the forest, Senonora, make one of his rare appearances by daylight. Senonora's name struck terror into the hearts of both man and beast, and Kgabo was full of excitement at the news. But the woman became more frightened than ever when he mentioned the matter to her, so he came to the conclusion that there was no truth in the rumour, and went upon *his* way.

Close upon the heels of the monkey came a string of other animals. Tshipo the spring-hare, Phudu-hudu the neat little steenbuck, followed by Mrs. Mosha the yellow ground squirrel, with her two children – while close upon *her* heels came her cousin Samane, the grey and white squirrel. This, however, was not the end, for Tshipa, the black and white civet-cat minced out of the bushes, with her tail looking like a bottle-brush as she held it at right-angles to her body. They *all* asked what had happened to their drinking water – and they all received the same reply. Some were angry, but others passed on without a word.

At last it seemed that the long procession of creatures had come to an end, and the poor woman gave a sigh of relief, for night was approaching, and she did not relish the hours of darkness ahead of her. But her relief was short lived, for out of the shadows stalked Ntché, the big black and white ostrich.

Now, among the people of this land, Ntché was credited with certain human powers, and normally the woman would have hailed him with relief; but her slight ray of hope vanished when she made ready to address him as, before she had time to so much as open her mouth, the big bird fixed her with his large evil eyes and hissed, "*Where is our water?*"

"My big stomach drank it," replied the unhappy woman fearfully, struggling to rise to her feet.

"Well, I did not make your big stomach," he continued in his cracked voice, "I came for a drink of water, because I happen to be thirsty, and I am not going away without it!" He thereupon raised his powerful long bare leg and slashed her stomach open with his sharp toe-nail so that all the water that she had drunk came gushing out to fill once more, the animals' drinking pool.

Ntché drank long and deeply, after which he left the woman where she had fallen and went upon his way, satisfied that he had given back to his fellow-creatures that which the woman had taken from them.

For many days the man waited in vain for the return of his wife, tending his little son as best he could; but he never saw her again for she was dead – killed by the hidden power of her tribal totem, the revenge of *Tawana*, the Lion Cub. Retribution had been meted out to one who had transgressed the "totem law". *It is finished*.*

Narrator: Mokgalagadi Seleka. Aged 85.

---

*There is nobody who can alter the outcome, for the totem of a tribe is all-powerful.

7

THE CROCODILE PRINCE

Masilo and his wife were very poor – but they were diligent, and regularly from morning until dusk they hoed and tilled their tidy garden. No couple in the whole of the drought-stricken area worked so hard as they, and they looked to their industry to bear a good harvest in the lean months ahead.

With this thought uppermost in mind, they sang cheerfully as they wended their way home each night. However, it was fortunate that they were in ignorance of the trouble that lay ahead, for they had hardly passed out of sight of their labours one evening, when a beautiful bird that shone copper and blue as the vanishing rays of sunlight glinted upon its exotic plumage, alighted upon a tree that grew beside their well-hoed land.

"Mix-up, mix-up, oh Masilo's land. Become uncultivated, Masilo's land!" it chanted in a loud, harsh voice – and immediately the work that the couple had toiled so diligently to complete, became undone, and nothing remained to greet them, when they returned to continue their hoeing on the following day, but the bare earth.

"What is *this*?" gasped Masilo in astonishment, as he and his wife came within sight of their previous day's labour. "Have we been so drugged with sleep overnight that we have followed the wrong path to our work, finding bare veld to greet us at its end?"

"No, my husband," the wife answered fearfully, "for see, our lazy neighbours' gardens are still upon either side. There, Ntsilwane's rough, unfinished pumpkin patch which he scratched but yesterday – and there the water-pot he left behind because it leaked!"

Neither Masilo nor his wife could understand this strange occurrence and, when their neighbours arrived not long afterwards and laughed at them for their laziness, they began to feel that they must surely have been overpowered by the drowsy sunshine of the previous day, and *dreamed* that they had worked so hard. Such disgraceful behaviour must not occur again! Therefore, they set to work with re-doubled energy, to make up for their imagined lapse.

Hot and tired after their exertions, the husband and wife hurried back to their hut that evening as the sun sank behind the distant horizon. But no sooner were they out of sight, than the same bird again alighted upon the tree beside Masilo's garden. "Mix-up, mix-up, oh Masilo's land. Become uncultivated, Masilo's land!" it chuckled mischievously. Again the carefully hoed earth became rough, grass-covered veld, and the bird flew away, happy in the damage it had caused, as the darkness once more descended over Masilo's untilled land.

There was fear as well as anger in the hearts of the man and woman when they reached their garden on the following day. "We have been bewitched!" they cried as they gazed at their once more grass-covered patch; "Someone surely has a grudge against us!"

On many days that followed, the same thing happened, until in despair Masilo planned to set a trap for the one who was causing so much mischief. Having done this, he sent his wife home ahead of him and, hiding in a hole that he had dug beneath the tree next to his plot, settled down to watch.

It was not long before the bird flew to the same perch as usual and immediately croaked, "Mix-up, mix-up, oh Masilo's land. Become uncultivated, Masilo's land!" and the man witnessed with his own eyes, all the hard work of his wife and himself become undone.

His mischief completed, the bird prepared to fly away. But it rose clumsily so, jumping upwards with all his strength, Masilo caught it by the legs. "Wicked one," he threatened, drawing his knife from his belt to kill it, "your days of sorcery are ended."

The bird wept bitterly, begging Masilo to spare its life.

"What! *Spare your life*, when you have done your best to kill us by slow starvation, in bringing our labours to naught?" the man scoffed. "Then let me see if you can *undo* the mischief that you have done, by *cultivating* my land once more – *and* grow a crop for me. Maybe you can be of greater use to me alive, than dead!"

At once the bird croaked, "Become cultivated, become cultivated, oh Masilo's land," and at once the plot passed from matted grass to a well-cared-for garden of crowing crops, at which Masilo clapped his hands with pleasure. "It is not only *this* that I can do for you, if you will spare me," boasted the bird, "I will make madila* for you to eat when you are hungry. All that you have to do is to take out the little plug that you will

---

*Curdled milk.

find above my tail, and name your wish." Masilo lost no time in doing this, and the wonderful bird poured forth enough curdled milk to satisfy his hunger and which, he found to his delight, was the most delicious food that he had ever tasted.

"It is well," the man exclaimed with pleasure. "I will take you home and make you work for me . . . "Wife!" he called out cheerfully as he came in sight of the hut, "Prepare our largest storage pot to receive a quantity of food."

"Fool," she answered bitterly, "what food is there in this starvation land? Satisfy our children's hunger, before you joke with me!" and she stamped angrily into the hut.

"Bring out the storage pots, I say! And be quick about it, if you wish to fill your children's empty stomachs," he scolded her. This time the woman did as she was bidden and Masilo, pulling the plug from above the bird's tail, commanded it to make madila for the family. At once the nourishing beverage gushed forth, until all were completely satisfied.

Masilo immediately began to construct a strong cage in which to keep his magic bird, forbidding his wife and children ever to touch it, or to share their precious secret with anyone.

As the weeks passed and the drought increased, Masilo and his family waxed fat, while those around them grew thinner by the day. "The man and wife are poor," the villagers whispered among themselves, "and yet, in spite of the fact that they have grown lazy of late, they appear to want for nothing; we must spy upon them, and learn the secret of their plenty." But try as they would, no one was able to unravel the mystery.

However, not only did Masilo and his wife become lazy, now that all their wants were provided for them, but they developed a taste for gaiety. Week after week they visited the neighbouring villages, leaving their children to care for themselves. True, they left them all the food that they could wish – provided by the magic bird – but the neglect by their parents filled the two children with resentment, with the result that one day they disobeyed their father's order, and took their little playmates into his hut to show off the provider of their plenty.

"Come, we will feast you!" boasted Masilo's son as he took the bird from its cage and held it, while his sister removed the magic plug as usual. The boy then bade it fill their vessels one by one with its magic liquid, and at once the flow gushed forth. Their guests gazed in astonishment as the bird filled one container after another with rich madila, and without waiting for a second invitation, they sat down to enjoy their unaccustomed treat.

As the last vessel filled, Masilo's son looked around him for the plug to stop the magic flow – but his sister could not remember where she had put it. She must have dropped it upon the floor, she thought; but although everyone helped in the search, the precious plug could not be found. Her brother tried to stop the flow of liquid with his finger, but could not, and the stream of madila poured on, and on.

Soon a thick white rivulet found its way through the open door to form a pool outside, and as the little visitors fled in consternation, the bird began to show signs of exhaustion until at last, utterly spent and worn, it fell dead at the feet of the boy and his sister.

Afraid to face their parents' anger upon their return, the brother and sister fled into the wilds, where, after travelling for many days, and undergoing great hardships, they came to a large and strangely dome-shaped rock. The boy tapped upon its rough surface saying sadly, "Rock, we are homeless and alone; please give us shelter." With a creak and a groan a crevice in the big rock opened and, squeezing their way inside the children found a space sufficiently large in which to live in comfort.

For several years the brother and sister lived in the peace and security of their rock home, and during this time the boy became an expert hunter. With his bow and arrows he provided meat for their daily needs, besides pelts and skins from which to fashion wraps and clothes against the winter cold. The nimble fingers of the girl wove sleeping mats and shaped the pots in which to cook their simple fare – and they were content in each other's companionship.

This easy, carefree life might well have lasted forever, had not the girl caught sight, while returning from the river one day with the daily water supply, of an enormous crocodile following in her footsteps. "Brother, brother!" she cried in terror, "Save me from the dreadful monster that has come to devour me!"

In response to her cries the boy ran to her aid and, hastily fitting an arrow to his bow, was about to send it humming on its journey when the crocodile called to him, "Do not kill me, human, for I wish to be your friend. Put down your bow and arrows, child, and I will take you to my home, where gifts await you."

Friends were few and far between for these two children, so they gladly accompanied the crocodile to his river home. Deep down beneath the water the creature guided the boy until, reaching an under-water kingdom, the strange reptile showed the lad his many possessions. "Take these cattle," he said, driving ten beautiful fat cows apart from the rest of the herd, "they are my gift to you."

The boy's eyes grew wide with wonder at his good fortune, and with the crocodile's help he drove the beasts up through the water to the dry land above. Their new friend then produced two large baskets full of millet, which he presented to the equally astonished girl.

But the young people's hearts sank as, after accepting their thanks the crocodile turned to the boy and said, "For these and future favours, I demand that you pledge your sister to be my bride."

With this dreadful thought to accompany them, the brother and sister drove the cattle to their rock home, where they built a stockade to protect the precious herd from the wild beasts around them. It was also not long after this that a plot of millet plants waved their heads in the soft breezes in a fertile clearing nearby.

From this time onward the crocodile bestowed great kindness upon the maturing youth and maid, until eventually they felt that he was necessary to their happiness, and they hailed him with pleasure instead of dread when he waddled his ungainly body up the now well-worn path between their homes.

"Sister," said the boy one day, after their reptile friend had been in deep conversation with him, "our friend the crocodile reminds us that the time is ripe to celebrate your marriage to him, according to our agreement. It is now that I must give you to him as his wife."

"It is well," replied the maiden, "I would wish for no other to be my lord and master. I am ready to obey his every wish."

"Then caress me, to prove your willingness, my Lovely One," the hideous creature ordered her, holding up his repulsive mask. At once she obeyed this, his first order, and immediately a wonderful change came over his reptile shape: his ugly features took on a human look, and he threw off his scaly covering, to stand before her as a Prince of both beauty and nobility.

"My father's enemies cast this wicked spell upon me," he said, his eyes shining with gratitude, "but your love and faith in me has overcome their wickedness."

Many years of happiness followed the marriage of the maid to the "Crocodile Prince", whose kingdom and all his people were also restored to him due to his wife's love and faith. And, although this could easily be the end of the story, we will go just a little further.

In the course of time another drought struck the homeland of the brother and sister, and this time it was so severe that its hungry people travelled far and wide to neighbouring kingdoms in search of food. And it so happened that one day there came to the home of the Crocodile Prince a starving man and his wife – and the brother and sister looked long and wistfully at the old couple. "Our father and our mother," they whispered to each other, "whose magic bird we caused to die. Hush, do not let them know that we are here, for they are surely happy to think us dead!"

At the request of his wife the Crocodile Prince gave the old couple as many baskets of grain as they could carry and, with some cattle by which to raise a herd once more, sent them to make a new home in a fertile valley nearby.

Here, the old couple lived in happiness and peace, until they were called to their forefathers at a ripe old age, without ever knowing that their long lost son and daughter were watching over their comfort.

8

THE SILVER TREE

In one of the dry and arid areas of Botswana, there lived a long time ago, a hard-working man and his wife. Although they were happy in each other's love, they shared a great sorrow, for no child had been born to them during their years of married life.

They were no longer young, and the work for their very existence in the barren area around them was falling heavily upon their shoulders. However, once more it was planting time, and unless they were prepared to starve during the year ahead, they must bestir themselves to sow their carefully hoarded stock of seeds in time to catch the early rains.

Carefully the husband scraped the hard earth, whilst his wife followed, sowing the seed ready for him to cover on the return trip. But, alas, as fast as the grain reached the ground, the birds flocked down from the skies and picked it up. This was indeed serious, for their remaining stock of seed was small.

For two days they endeavoured to plant the grain; once, twice, *three* times a day – but the birds gave them no peace, swarming down on each occasion to clean it up ere it was covered. At last the husband said with a sigh of resignation, "Wife, it is useless for us to waste our time, for soon there will be no seed left to plant. Let us wait until the burning heat of midday has arrived, when the birds will be less active while they shelter from the sun."

"Husband, you are right," replied the wife, "we will start again at midday." But as they were upon the point of returning to their home, a white-necked crow alighted nearby and addressed the wife saying, "Woman, my friends are hungry; do not grudge them the corn that is left to you. Feed it to the feathered ones, and good fortune shall be your reward."

"My reward will be starvation in the months to come," replied the woman grudgingly. "How could it be otherwise? With no seed left to plant, we will surely die!"

"Yet I do assure you that it shall be otherwise," said the crow mysteriously. "I can say no more than that great happiness will come to both of you, should you carry out my wish!"

As soon as the cloud of birds had risen from their feast, the crow approached the couple and said, "Thank you for feeding my friends. Your reward shall be in keeping with your kindness. Now, you must listen carefully to what I have to say. First prepare a feast by killing your most treasured ox; remove the stomach and entrails from it; clean out the dung, but do not throw it away – this must be burned with care, and the ashes placed in the centre of your yard. Next call up your neighbours from near and far, and bid them share the spread with you.

"The rest of my instructions are *most* important. Take the horns, entrails, stomach and feet – also the heart, liver, kidneys and lungs. Count them with care – eight items in all. Bind these within the skin so that air can get neither in nor out: place the bundle inside your hut, and leave the door ajar.

"This, too, my friends, you must carry out with care. *Whatever you hear* you must not close the door, nor must you kindle any light, nor interfere with anything that is taking place, until the crowing of the cock heralds the new-born day."

After this long speech the crow flew away, leaving the husband and wife sorely perplexed and ill at ease, for they were simple folk, who felt that such instructions were greatly beyond their understanding. However, having already parted with the remainder of their precious grain, they felt that they would be foolish not to listen to the crow, so they did as the bird had bade them with the utmost care.

When the guests had eaten well of the sumptuous repast thus provided for them, they returned to their homes, while the husband and wife retired for the night, leaving the door of their hut ajar as instructed by the crow. But, curiosity having driven all thoughts of sleep from them, they lay peering into the darkness for what seemed an eternity.

However, it cannot have been more than an hour or two before they heard a slight rustling at the door, and it seemed as though a gentle breeze blew in; then there was silence once more. But presently, from the direction of the trussed-up skin, they heard sounds akin to groans and mumbling.

The old couple clutched each other in fear in the darkness, but remembering the crow's warning, they uttered not a sound. Then, in the deep silence of the night they heard a voice say clearly, "Stomach, move over – give me more room!" Then another voice broke in, "Feet, you are treading on me – move over!" Then once more another voice interrupted, "Horns, you are pricking me!" and thus, throughout the darkness the "voices" went on, while the husband and wife clung together upon their sleeping mat . . . too afraid to move.

At last, with a shrill crow, the cock announced the coming day, and the old couple crept shakily onto their knees, wondering what would confront them, as they rose to approach the skin. "What magic is this?" cried the husband in fear, as he saw the bundle heave and move, whereupon he slashed it open with his knife.

Sighs of relief greeted his action as, one by one, eight lovely children climbed out of their ox-skin prison. "Thank you for letting us out," they said, and pointing to the skin added, "for there was very little room for so many of us in there!"

The husband and wife fell upon their faces in gratitude, for they realised that this was their reward for giving the last of their grain to the starving birds. But this was not all. There was another surprise in store for them, for when they went into the yard they found that where they had placed the ashes of the dung the night before, there stood a beautiful Silver Tree, laden with luscious fruit, and in its branches sat their friend the crow.

"The fruit of this tree," said the bird, "is to be eaten by you and your children alone, but do not forget your friends the birds. All the seeds that are cast from the fruit must be saved, and scattered upon the land for them."

"Surely," said the old couple to each other, "this is little enough for our friend the crow to ask, in exchange for so many lovely sons and daughters!"

The husband and wife faithfully carried out the pledge that they at once made, and there was no need for them ever again to sow their lands, for the Silver Tree provided ample food for them all – including their friends the birds.

Narrator: Botsile Molokela.

9

LERUARUA

"Hush, hush, Little Sweetness," Sebotshe* begged her baby sister, as she hitched the braided tharing,† in which she carried the child, higher upon her back, and tried to soothe the little one by the swaying motion of her body.

The parents of the two children were dead, and the baby still pined for the gentle care of her mother; she refused to be comforted, and her screams continued to rend the peace and quietude around them.

" 'The-one-whose-name-we-will-not-speak' will hear your cries, and we will *both* be beaten," implored the elder girl, but Sebotshane** would not cease her bawling, so Sebotshe plucked a shoot from the Thathamora-thwa†† tree that grew in her guardian's yard and, putting it into the baby's mouth said soothingly, "There, there, Little Sweetness, may the Tree of Comfort enable you to forget your sorrow!"

At once there was a contented silence. But the sudden quietude had anything but the desired effect, for the figure of their guardian appeared in the doorway of his hut, and he asked what had made the child cease her crying in such an unexpected manner.

"I did but give her a shoot from the 'Tree of Comfort' to suck, and it has silenced her, my uncle," replied Sebotshe.

"And who," he asked angrily, "gave you authority to touch the tree in my yard?"

Although little Sebotshe felt a trifle nervous at the tone of her uncle's voice, she answered without hesitation, for she was a truthful child, "None told me that I may, but also none told me that I may not. How should I know that I was doing wrong?"

"Silence, child!" the uncle stormed. "You have disobeyed my *wishes*, if not my orders, so you must suffer. Come, I will take you to visit one whose magic will spoil that pretty face of yours." And, driving her before

---

*Sweetness.
†Carrying skin.
**Little sweetness.
††The Tree of Comfort.

him, he took her towards the home of Maké, a witch-doctor of ill repute, who lived many kilometres away.

From time to time they passed travellers on the way and all, being struck by the look of sadness upon the face of the lovely child, asked, "Friend, to where do you travel in such haste, driving one of such wondrous beauty before you?"

To each the uncle made the same reply, "I am taking my brother's child to one who has no use for pretty faces. To one who is well-known as 'The Spoiler of Beauty', that he may disfigure her loveliness, for she has disobeyed her guardian's wishes."

To each questioner the child cried out in anguish, "No, no, do not believe his cruel falsehood! I did not disobey; I only picked a shoot from the Tree of Comfort to pacify my little sister. Was it wrong to turn her sorrow into gladness?"

Each time she tried to tell her story, the uncle drove her on, calling out angrily, "Do not listen to her childish lies. I tell you, she deserves the fate I have in store for her."

As their journey drew near to its end, little Sebotshe grew more and more frightened at the thought of what might lie ahead for her, and she was near to tears when they met a chief and his son with their retinue, returning from a visit to their neighbours.

Seeing Sebotshe's beauty, the chief turned to one of his followers and said, "Surely this child is of gentle birth, and should not be treated as a slave. Ask her keeper what makes him travel at such speed, driving one so young and beautiful before him?"

To the chief's messenger the uncle made the same reply as he had made to those before him, but this time Sebotshe cried louder than before, "Do not believe him; I did not disobey!" and again she repeated her story.

"Father," said the chief's son, "I fear for the life of this lovely child. Let me take her for my wife." The chief listened with compassion to his son's request, and negotiations were at once entered into, whereby the cruel uncle, delighted with his bargain, handed Sebotshe over to the old chief, in payment of many fat cattle as a bride price, to swell his precious herd.

When the time became ripe, a splendid wedding was celebrated, after which the happy bride and bridegroom settled down in the old chief's kraal.

All was feasting and merriment throughout the village when a son was eventually born to the young couple. They called him Tlhako ya Pitse*, and in his joy the old chief gave the mother and father sufficient cattle, sheep and goats, besides followers and land, to found a village of their own. In high good spirits the young chief's people collected their herds and flocks one beautiful sunny day, and together left their old surroundings to choose a site on which to build their new home.

For many miles they travelled, until finally they reached a large river "There should be good pastures for our beasts beyond these waters," said the young chief as the men congregated upon the bank ready to drive the beasts across. But to their dismay the water parted as a huge head rose out of it, and the dreaded monster, Leruarua, scrambled towards them. Baring its enormous jagged teeth it made straight for Sebotshe and said in a menacing voice, "I am going to eat you, mother of Tlhako ya Pitse!"

The little mother looked around her in terror and distress, as she thought of the babe she carried upon her back. "Do not eat *me* good Leruarua," she begged, "pray eat the flocks and herds instead!" and she gave a sigh of relief as the creature opened its cavernous mouth in obedience to her wish, and swallowed the livestock one by one.

However, her relief was but short-lived for, as the last struggling beast went down its throat the monster, now enlarged beyond all imagining, came again to Sebotshe's side and repeated its horrid threat, "I am going to *eat* you, mother of Tlhako ya Pitse," and its huge white teeth flashed in the sunshine.

"Do not eat me, oh, please do not eat me!" begged Sebotshe: "Pray eat the people instead!" and the monster obediently gulped down the young couple's followers one by one, until only their three selves were left.

Her fear increased as Leruarua, still not satisfied after this tremendous meal, advanced again upon them; but it was once more to the little mother that he addressed his repeated threat, "I am going to eat you, mother of Tlhako ya Pitse!"

Sebotshe covered her eyes with her two hands, so that she should not see the sight that she knew would greet her next for, still hoping to save her little son she said, "Do not eat me, good Leruarua, please eat Pitse's father instead!"

*Hoof of a zebra.

For the third time the monster obeyed her wish, and she sobbed as she realised that her beloved husband had gone to join his beasts and followers – and she and her baby were left on the bank alone. Surely Leruarua must be satisfied, and would spare them now that she had sacrificed all that had made life sweet, in order that her little one should not be left without her guiding hand.

But now came the biggest test of all. Her terror mounted even higher as she watched Leruarua, *still* not satisfied, approach her for the fourth time. "I am going to eat you, mother of Tlhako ya Pitse," it repeated, with an evil look in its bloodshot eyes and, opening a cavernous mouth, prepared to gulp her down.

"No, no!" the mother cried in wild despair, looking around for some means of escape. Better surely, she thought, that her son should join the rest – for at least his end would be quick, and he would not be left alone – so she answered as she held up the child to him, "Please do not eat me; eat my little one instead!" and the monster swallowed Pitse.

"This time *nothing* will save you, mother of Tlhako ya Pitse, for you have sacrificed all, that you may live – *I am going to eat you!*" hissed the monster as it came at her.

But she met it bravely this time, and smiled as the enormous jaws closed upon her, for she had snatched a spear which lay half hidden in the grass at her feet. Fortunately the spear was very sharp, so, as she went down Leruarua's enormous throat, she ripped the creature open from head to tail.

Out tumbled the cows with their calves, the sheep with their lambs, the goats with their kids, the frogs with their young – in fact every other thing that had been eaten that day, including the women with their husbands and children, the young chief with their little son and, last of all, herself.

"You have saved us, mother of Pitse – you have saved us!" they one and all cried joyfully. "We owe our lives to you. You are from now on, the mother of us all!"

With the dreaded Leruarua now dead, they had nothing more to fear, so they built their village near to the place where the monster had died, in honour of the young mother whose love for her little son had unwittingly saved them all from a dreadful fate.

Narrator: Mmanito Kepidisa. Aged 85.

10

MONYENYANE AND THE FALCON

Fragile and fairylike was Monyenyane, the little Tswana girl – so named after the dainty, soft, short vlei grasses that danced their delicate white flowers up and down in the breezes. So beautiful was she in fact, that everyone who saw her came to love her. This was very delightful to be sure, but it turned her happiness into sorrow when her own brother fell deeply in love with her sweetness.

"Brother," she sighed sadly, "I must leave our home forever, and we must never meet again."

In the stillness of the night that followed, Monyenyane crept silently from the home she loved so dearly, and vanished into the shadows of the moonlit veld. Mile upon mile she trudged, following the path of the sinking moon until to her great relief she saw a glimmer of light in the far distance, and made for its friendly twinkle.

She tapped softly upon the rush mat that hung across the doorway of a small hut, and was answered by a woman's voice that asked her business. "I have no business," replied Monyenyane, "but I come from afar, and wander in a strange land."

"Come in," the woman invited her, "for your voice sounds as pure and sweet to the ear as rippling waters upon fern banks. Come in, my child!"

Stooping, Monyenyane pushed aside the rush mat and made her way into the hut. There she found an old, old woman hunched against the wall.
"Do not touch me, breath of sweetness," sighed the old crone, "for my sorrows have brought me near to death." She bared her wounded side which, she told the girl, had been eaten by her dimo* son. "He will come again tonight," the old woman added in a resigned voice, "and when he knocks you must refuse to let him in; say to him, 'the meat is not yet fit to eat'; and he will go away."

Monyenyane slept but fitfully throughout the remaining hours of darkness and, hearing the dimo demand admittance later on, she answered as she had been instructed by the old woman – and was relieved to hear

*Cannibal.

him go away. But on the following morning when she was about to depart upon her journey the old woman, feeling that her end was drawing near, and wishing to avenge her injuries upon her unnatural son, begged the girl to stay for the coming night, to assist her in her plans.

Monyenyane readily agreed to carry out the woman's wishes after she had listened to them, and she sat up when darkness came, to trick the dimo upon his arrival. Hour upon hour she waited for him until, overcome by sleep she fell into a fitful doze. She awakened with a start to find the old woman gone, and the hut filled with hurrying shapes; Tau and his cruel brother lions had come, at the dimo's invitation, for a human feast.

Picking up Monyenyane in his powerful jaws, Tau carried her out of the hut into the gloom of the forest, where he put her down. Setting a circle of his friends to guard her, he planned to enjoy a feast at his leisure in the morning.

But Monyenyane's namesakes, the dainty veld grasses, wafted their sleep-inducing fragrance into the nostrils of her guards until, drugged by its power, they slept. The dew, whose name she likewise shared, also came silently to her assistance and damped the path upon which she trod, causing her footsteps to fall more softly – and while the circle of her captors slumbered, Monyenyane once more stole into the night . . . and away.

The gentle creatures of the forest looked pityingly at her as she hastened past them, for they knew the merciless persistence of the cruel Tau, and how he and his friends would cunningly track her foot-prints until they had the child in their toils once more.

Sure enough, when upon waking, the lions found that their prey had disappeared, they lost no time in following her trail, and soon caught up with her as she fled. They were about to drag her to the ground when, in her terror, she climbed to the highest branches of a tree, where she was safe from their tearing claws.

The lions, however, had no intention of allowing their prospective feast to escape in such an easy manner, so they settled round the base of the tree to starve her into coming down. This they would probably have succeeded in doing, had not Monyenyane seen Segwetsane, the yellow falcon, hovering high in the sky above her, and called loudly to him for help.

Great was her relief, but greater still the lions' anger when Segwetsane swooped down from the heights in answer to the maiden's cry, to pluck

her from her refuge in the treetop. Then far, far away the falcon bore her – back to the land of human habitations, and there he put "the little grass-flower" down upon the bank of a river.

It so happened that the son of the ruling chief of that land was watering his father's flocks and herds at a nearby pool, and he shaded his eyes with a hand as he watched the noble bird descend from the skies – and he gasped with astonishment when he realised what a lovely load Segwetsane carried. "Father!" he cried, as he arrived breathless at the door of the old chief's hut shortly after, "the good bird Segwetsane has brought me a bride of wondrous fairness, straight from the very Gates of Heaven! Come, I will take you to her."

The boy led the old man to where the falcon had left Monyenyane at the edge of the water. The chief was delighted at the fairy-like beauty of the girl, and at once agreed that she would indeed be a fitting bride for the heir to so vast a kingdom as his own.

It was with a feeling of great happiness and relief that the girl found herself among such kind and understanding people, after her frightening experiences and, being resolved never again to put temptation in her beloved brother's way by returning to her home, she gladly accepted their hospitality. Day by day the love of the chief's son for her grew, until, amid celebrations of great splendour, the marriage of the boy and girl took place.

The kindness of the good falcon was not forgotten in the years that followed for, when a baby girl was born to them, they named her Senonyane*, in memory of the bird who saved the life of her beloved mother.

Narrator: Elizabeth Matlanyane.

---

*Nonyane is the generic term for bird.

11

SELEKANE

Dainty, good-natured Selekane was the last to reach the river with her water-pot balanced upon her head, only to find that her cousins had already drawn their brimming pots from the clear waters of the pool, and were about to leave upon the return journey.

Before her arrival one of the girls had said, "Let us hide our beads and ornaments beneath the sand, and when our cousin comes we will tell her that we have thrown them into the pool as an offering to The Spirit of the River. She will then do likewise, and we can laugh at her expense. Maybe it will teach her not to linger at the village as she does."

Quickly they had hidden their beaded ornaments near to the water's edge, and had hardly completed their deception before Selekane arrived breathless from her haste. "Cousins," she smiled, "you have been very quick today; I was delayed . . . " (she omitted to add that she had stayed behind to help an old cripple with her household chores) and she dipped *her* vessel into the clear, cool water.

"Yes," replied the eldest girl, "we hastened because The Spirit of the River demanded that we sacrifice our beads and trinkets to him as an offering for future favours. See, we have thrown ours into the water – and should *you* wish for protection against one who devours lovely maidens, we would advise you to do the same!"

Selekane looked first at their unadorned bodies, and then lovingly at her pretty beads and shining bangles. They were her greatest treasures. Only *very* treasured daughters were decked as lavishly as she. But she was a trusting child, and it would never do, she decided, to insult The Spirit of the River by refusing to follow her cousins' example! So reluctantly she pulled her lovely beads and necklets from her body and, not daring to look at them in case she weakened, cast them far into the silent pool.

Her action was greeted by a burst of laughter from the group of girls, as they rushed to the hiding place to uncover the bangles and strings of precious beads. "Fool!" they giggled, "Was it only yesterday that you left your mother's breast? Who after this, will be so foolish as to decorate your naked body once more?" and, swinging their water-pots onto their heads they hurried home, much amused and leaving Selekane gazing horror-stricken into the silent pool.

"Noka*, ah Noka!" she sobbed, "Give me back my lovely beads, I beg of you!" but never a ripple showed upon the glassy surface of the pool, so she cried again, "Noka, Noka, oh *please* Noka, restore my lovely beads to me."

This time there was a slight disturbance as the water parted and a voice came from out of it which said, "Follow me; follow my ripples, if you would find them."

She ran hopefully along the bank until she came to a very much larger and deeper pool where she stopped and called again, "Noka, ah! Please, Noka, return my beads to me!"

Once more there was no reply so, after a further pause she repeated her request for the third time, and immediately there was a violent eruption of the water as a louder voice answered, "Sister, *come and get them!*"

Submerging herself in the water Selekane sank down, down, down, until she reached the bottom of the pool where, groping about in the semi-darkness, she found herself at the entrance to a large and brightly lighted cave. She walked in timidly, to be greeted by an ugly old woman who bounded towards her in enormous hops, and Selekane saw with horror that the poor creature's right arm and leg were missing.

Three hops brought the old hag to the girl's side; "Ngwanaka†," she whined, "is not the sight of one as old and repulsive as I, distasteful to you? Come, laugh at my misfortunes!"

"Dumela Mma**," the girl answered. "How can I laugh when my heart is full of anger against those who have brought such trouble upon you?"

"If the sight of me does not repulse you, my child, then let the balm of your softly spoken tongue heal my wounds by licking them," the old crone begged.

Selekane did as the woman requested, whereupon the old hag caressed her saying, "Child, you have a compassionate heart as well as a lovely face; I will reward you.

*River.
†My child.
**Good morning, grandmother.

"I have been imprisoned in this cave for many years by the cruel Kwena,* in order that I should care for him and do his bidding. So that I shall not escape from his clutches he has maimed me thus, but I shall save you from him. Eat, my pretty one," she encouraged Selekane, placing food in front of her, "and when you have satisfied your hunger, I shall hide you, for soon you will hear the sound of pattering raindrops falling, followed by the noise of rushing waters, which always herald my master's approach."

Presently the old woman hopped to her side to hurry the girl into an adjoining cave as they heard the dreaded noise that she had predicted, and no sooner was she hidden than a hideous crocodile waddled into sight. His untidy ginger scales hung loosely about his crouched, misshapen body, and between his yellow, protruding lips there stuck out unevenly a row of enormous moss-covered teeth. "Hmmmm," he chuckled, licking his dreadful jowls, "I smell human flesh and blood! Cook it for me, woman, for I am hungry."

"Then your hunger must go unsatisfied," the woman answered bravely, "unless you wish to eat my remaining leg and arm. But such would avail you nothing, for who would cater for your needs *if I should die?* I tell you, it is your *own* blood that pollutes your nostrils, for it is plain to me that you have fought this day!" and she pointed to a large gash on the side of his head, upon which the blood had caked and dried.

After an unsuccessful search during which he tortured the woman to try to make her reveal the hiding place of his hoped-for victim, the crocodile went to sleep grumbling, assuring her that he would most certainly eat her if he found that she had lied to him.

"Child," said the old woman, calling the girl from her hiding place as soon as the creature had left the cave on the following morning, "it is my wish to reward you for restoring to me my faith in human kindness." She rummaged among some old rags and skins in a crevice in the wall, to pull out of it a pile of beaded ornaments. These she hung about Selekane's neck and waist, then added bangles to decorate her arms and legs – while a skirt of softest calf-skin was followed by a wrap of jackal-skin to put about her lovely body.

"Now," the woman smiled, surveying her handiwork with undisguised

*Crocodile.

pleasure, "you must leave this under-water cavern with the utmost haste, before my master returns (as I know he will, to see if I have tricked him), and may good fortune attend you, child." She drew a glittering green stone from amongst her ragged garments and, handing it to the girl added, "Take this amulet, for it will make my master powerless to follow you as long as it is in your hand. When you reach the pool where your cruel cousins tricked you, throw it far into the water's depths, and it will return to me."

Thanking her for her kindness, Selekane left the old woman and reached the pool without adventure. "Mai!" exclaimed her mother's youngest child, who happened to be at that very moment dipping her pot into the water, "What lovely maiden is *this* who visits our pool uninvited? Why, sister," she cried in surprise, "we have looked upon you as dead since our cousins assured us that The Spirit of the River had swallowed you. But *is* it you? For surely such trappings are the possessions of royalty alone!"

"Nevertheless, I do assure you that it *is* I," replied Selekane. "These coverings are a gift from one whose dwelling is a cave, deep beneath the water. They were given to me in acknowledgement of my offerings to The Spirit of the River, whom our cousins slighted yesterday."

There was both excitement and jealousy when the sisters reached their mother's hut and Selekane had told her tale, although she modestly refrained from telling of her kindness to the disfigured old woman.

"Come," said the cousins one to the other shortly afterwards, "why should Selekane have *all* the favours? Let us also benefit from the goodwill of The Spirit of the River. *We* will visit the magic cave, and reap from its store of riches. They dressed themselves in their best attire and, hurrying to the river, threw their trinkets far into the pool as Selekane had done. Then, following the same procedure, they scrambled into the big pool, where they soon found the underwater cave.

The crippled old woman at once hopped forward to meet them – but they laughed at her misfortune, and avoided the grasp of her skinny hand. "Beads, beads," they clamoured. "We have come for *beads*."

"Daughters," she besought them, "have pity upon me. My sores have brought me near to death; lick them clean, that the magical properties of your tongues may heal them!"

"What! Lick your filthy sores?" they screamed. "We have come for *beads*. Give us the trinkets for which we came, and be quick about it, that we may leave this place of horrors."

"Not so fast!" the old woman cautioned. "I see that your hearts are even blacker than your faces. Today my master shall truly eat his fill." And as a great shadow cast a darkness across the entrance to the cave, they heard the patter of raindrops falling, and the sound of rushing water . . . and, hopping from the girls' view, the old woman left them to their fate.

12

THE LION AND THE HARE

It is said among the people of the Bamangwato tribe, that once upon a time long, long ago, Tau the lion walked alone throughout the land until finally he met Mmutla, the hare.

"Here is the King of the Beasts," thought the wily hare. "I will pit my wits against those of his lordship. "Good-day to you, Great One," he said ingratiatingly, "it is surely a sorrowful being who walks alone and without companionship upon Modimo's* good earth. May I be allowed to accompany you upon your travels?"

The lion grunted, and fixed the stare of his yellow eyes upon the hare, but remained silent.

"Is it not beneath the dignity of one of *your* high standing to do the menial tasks of the home?" persisted Mmutla. "Allow me the honour to do your cooking, and to run your daily errands."

Tau considered the matter for a few seconds. It would certainly be very pleasant, he decided, to hand over his household chores to one reputed to be as domesticated as the hare. "Very well," he agreed. "*I* will provide the food, while *you* shall both cook it and attend to the matters of the home. But mind, no roguery!"

"You misjudge me, my good uncle," smirked the hare with a touch of familiarity, "for it is well-known among the Forest Folk that none can run a home as well as I, nor cook such tasty food."

The lion thereupon led Mmutla to his retreat in a tangle of bushes, but the little creature looked around in horror at the general discomfort of his master's abode. "We must build a hut," he said, "to shelter us from the inclemencies of the weather."

"An excellent idea!" beamed the lion good-naturedly. "We will set to work at once."

For several days the two animals gathered material for their dwelling, after which they rammed the saplings into the ground before bending them over to form the roof. They worked hard, and soon began to cover

*The Great One.

the structure with thatching grass. In and out they pushed the long wooden needle, binding the grass firmly to the slender poles.

"Uncle, I am hungry," grumbled the hare one day when the work had nearly been completed. "Our meat is cooked – shall we not eat it before it spoils?"

"No," refused the lion. "*You* are the servant. *I* am the master. We shall eat when our work is done."

The lion was working on the top of the hut, while the hare pushed the thatching needle up through the grass to him. Mmutla carefully awaited his opportunity and, when it came, he looped the twine over Tau's paw binding it firmly to the roof. Tau roared with pain and anger, but Mmutla only jeered at him as he sat down alone to his repast. "As I remarked a short while ago, uncle," he sniggered, "our dinner is cooked to a turn. I am sorry you are not able to join me. Ha, ha, ha!" and while Tau struggled fruitlessly to free himself, the hare finished the pot of food.

However, the twine that bound the lion's foot eventually broke, so he sprang down from the roof and with a roar of indignation, bounded in pursuit of the fleeing hare. After a long chase he overtook Mmutla, and caught hold of one of his legs as he vanished down a hole. Holding to a root inside the hole so that Tau could not pull him out, the hare shouted. "You will never get me out *that* way, uncle. You are pulling on a root, instead of my leg!"

The lion immediately moved his grasp to the root that lay alongside the hare's leg and, with many sounds of merriment, Mmutla escaped further down the hole, to come out at an exit some distance away. "Uncle," he laughed, "it *was* kind of you to let me go like that!" and he skipped off, leaving the disappointed and angry lion to renew the chase.

It was some time before Tau gained upon him, but finally the hare came to a swiftly flowing river which completely barred his escape, and the lion managed to catch him. "Mighty One," sobbed the hare, "do what you like with me – kill me if you wish – but don't, oh *please* don't throw me across the river into my enemy's territory. *Anything* but that!"

"Aha!" chuckled Tau, "What greater punishment than the one he dreads so much?" and he hurled the hare with all his might across the water.

Tucking his feet beneath him as he sped through the air, Mmutla landed gracefully upon the other side of the river and, with a burst of laughter

made fun of the lion for helping him upon his way. However, Tau, seeing a log of wood drifting past in the water, quickly jumped upon it and, paddling it across to the opposite bank, caught the hare unawares, while he was still doubled-up with mirth.

"This time, my friend," said Tau, "I am going to *eat you* – for you will

remember that you ate my lunch a short while ago, and in consequence I am hungry."

The hare looked around him in despair. He must get himself out of this fix into which his mischief had landed him – but how? Glancing upwards he caught sight of a swarm of bees that happened to be hanging from one of the branches of the tree under which he had landed. "I admit, my good uncle," he replied, "that such a punishment is justified; but do not forget that it is customary to give thanks before you eat."

The lion obediently closed his eyes in benediction and the hare, hastily grabbing a stone, threw it into the midst of the clump of bees. There was an angry hum as the insects flew down to attack the cause of their disturbance.

Mmutla lost no time in disappearing into the long grass as, with a roar of pain the lion put his paws up to protect his eyes. However, these were soon so puffed from the many stings they had already received, that it was several days before he could see well enough to continue the hunt for his persecutor. "I will catch that rascally hare," he grumbled as he nursed his stings, "no matter how long I have to wait."

Opportunity came his way again about a week later when he happened to see Mmutla, drugged by the summer sun, lying asleep at the foot of a cliff. Silently and stealthily the big cat crept up to the sleeping hare; but quickly though he jumped, Mmutla's seventh sense saved him, for he awoke and jumped faster. Like a little streak of lightning, he reached the eaves of an overhanging rock, with the lion close upon his heels. "Quickly!" he shouted, "The rock is falling upon us. Help me to hold it up, my good uncle, or we will both be killed!"

The slow-thinking lion raised his paws to the overhanging rock and pushed with all his might.

"Whatever happens, don't let go, uncle, or you will most certainly be crushed," warned Mmutla as, with an impertinent tweak of Tau's tail as he passed, he ran off with a hop, skip and a jump into the safety of the forest.

It was a long, long time before Tau realised that he had once more been tricked, but by that time the wicked hare had wisely left the area, so Tau the lion continued to search for him in vain.

Narrator: Mmanito Kepidisa. Aged 85.

13

MATONG AND THE BIG BLACK OX

If only our minds of today could look far enough back into the dim distant past we might believe, as do the Bantu People, that once upon a time animals and humans talked to one another. In fact, in the present-day language of the Setswana people, to whom this story belongs, some animals are still classified as human beings. Therefore, what may seem strange to us today, was an ordinary occurrence long, long ago.

At the particular time of which I write there lived with his widowed mother, a young Motswana boy named Matong. Although the mother and son were poor, they owned one greatly prized possession – a beautiful black ox – and no matter how often they hungered, the mother would not part with this animal in spite of the fact that many of her neighbours had tried to buy him from her.

Her son and the ox had grown from babyhood and calf-hood together, and when Matong took the big beast out to graze, he rode proudly astride the animal's broad and glossy back, so that these two grew to love each other dearly.

But there came a time when Matong's mother fell ill and, fearing that her end was drawing near, she called Matong to her and said, "My child, when I die, which may come to pass before long, you will be left, alone in the world. Now, whatever happens you must never, never *ever* part with our friend the big black ox for, as you have seen for yourself, he is by no means an ordinary beast. He will be both a father and a mother to you. And should danger threaten, he will warn you of it, and will advise you what to do."

The woman became worse, and before she died again called Matong to her. This time she told him to gather together his few possessions and to go to his father's brother who lived a long day's journey from them, taking the black ox with him. "And, my child," she reminded him as he left, "remember my parting words; *the ox will be both a father and a mother to you* in the years to come."

When he came to the end of his journey, Matong found that his uncle had a son of his own age, who willingly agreed to share his hut with his

orphan cousin. And because Matong remembered his mother's last words, he rose early each day to seek good pastures for his beloved ox.

Although they pretended to welcome the boy, the uncle and aunt were angered that he made yet another mouth to feed, for they were also poor – and Matong was still too young to earn the food he ate. But there was his ox: surely they could sell the beast and use the money to ease this extra burden upon their shoulders, for of what use was the animal to anyone? He gave no milk, nor did he do anything towards providing for his little master's keep.

Before long had passed, they approached Matong with regard to the disposal of his precious possession. To their surprise and annoyance the boy stubbornly refused to agree to their suggestion. But as time went on and their needs grew greater, the uncle and aunt approached the boy again. He still refused, however, saying more firmly than ever, "No, you may *not* sell or kill my ox, because he is both my father and my mother." So, becoming desperate, they planned to kill the boy while he slept.

That evening while Matong was putting his ox in the little stone kraal that he had built, the faithful animal said, "Little master, you are in great danger: when you go to bed tonight, put your sleeping mat away from the door, on the *far* side of your cousin."

Matong did as the ox advised and, as soon as it was light upon the following morning, ran as usual to greet his four-legged friend who at once said to him, "Little master, the danger has not fully passed. While you slept last night, your cousin was killed in mistake for you. When your uncle discovers what he has done, he will try to kill us both; but if you will listen carefully to my instructions, we shall both be safe.

"Quickly cut a stout stick from the tree under which we stand, (but do not beat me with it!) Hold it in your hand, and on no account must you ever lose it. With your free hand you must then tightly grasp my tail, and together we will escape from here."

Matong had barely finished cutting the stick as instructed by the ox, when his uncle and aunt came out of their hut. Seeing their nephew alive and well, they realised that by mistake they must surely have killed their son. Full of remorse and bitterness at what they had done, they at once tried to catch Matong. But the big ox bolted, with the boy holding firmly to his tail. Owing to the speed with which they covered the ground, the aunt and uncle were soon left far behind, and it was not long before they gave up the chase.

When the boy and ox had travelled for some miles they came to a herd of cattle, out of which a big red bull came forth to challenge the strange intruder. The ox now told Matong that he wished to fight and overcome the strange bull. Therefore, the boy stood aside whilst a great battle was fought in which much blood was shed on either side, until finally the black ox gained a victory, and the red bull was killed.

The two continued their journey, and had covered a further distance when they came to a herd of dun-coloured cattle. The big black ox, already tired from his previous fight, said to his young master, "Here I will fight and die! But take heed of my last words to you; when I am dead, you must remove my skin with care, but on no account must you eat my flesh. Keep my skin with you *always*, and if ever you should want for anything, take this stick and gently beat my shrivelled hide. Your every need will at once be fulfilled."

The dun-coloured herd then came down in force upon the valiant ox, which was soon overcome and killed. Tearfully Matong skinned his beloved friend and, remembering the animal's last words he took the skin, leaving the carcass behind. Continuing once more upon his journey, he came to a village where he was received with kindness, and was offered some work in payment for his keep.

In return for this security the chief allowed the boy to tend his flocks and herds, taking them to pasture each day when the dew was off the grass. Returning at sunset, Matong would put his charges into their kraal then, sitting quietly apart, listen to the gossip, the daily news, and the general chatter around the fire in his master's hut. In this manner, he learned the happenings of each day.

The chief had a lovely daughter called Madikonyana whom, from the first day upon which he had seen her, Matong had loved. And as the years passed, so did this youth's love for the girl grow: but, poor orphan that he was, he had to stand aside while others sought her hand.

Because of her great beauty and her happy nature, Madikonyana had many admirers – so many in fact, that her father decided to stage a competition for her hand, among those who wished to wed her. Those were the days of the racing ox, when proud chiefs vied with one another for possession not only of the fleetest, but the strongest racing ox – the one that could clear the greatest obstacle, with a rider upon his back.

Word of the competition soon spread far afield, and hopeful entrants trained their favourite steeds, while Madikonyana's father ordered the digging of a broad, deep trench, over which the victorious ox and rider were required to leap. And as the great day approached, the excitement grew, and grew, and *grew*.

Each evening when Matong returned with the flocks and herds, he listened with increasing despondency to the chief's subjects discussing the coming contest, and daily the pain in his heart grew greater, as the thought of Madikonyana's approaching marriage. Two nights before the day of the competition he went to his hut feeling more depressed than ever: and as he approached the little mat upon which he slept, dreading the hours of darkness that lay before him, his eyes were drawn, as if by magnetism, to the skin of the big black ox where it rested stiff and dry, against the wall – and he remembered the last instructions of his faithful friend.

Taking the skin and his stick with him, Matong drove the chief's cattle farther than usual upon the following day and, leaving them to graze took the skin and gently beat it with the stick, saying as he did so, "Please, oh skin, give me a home befitting a high-born maid, and the best riding-ox in the land!"

The words had scarcely left his lips before there appeared in front of him a beautiful hut, and a pitch black ox closely resembling his companion of old. All that day he rode this beautiful animal, testing his paces, and putting him over all kinds of obstacles, until ox and rider moved as one. That night he sat happily beside the fire, listening to the plans for the great event.

When the following day dawned, all was bustle and excitement as the preparations for the contest were completed. From the youngest to the oldest woman, each donned a freshly braided skirt of skin and beads; heads were shaven, leaving only a small round growth of hair on top, and this was rubbed with fat and powdered mica until it shone and glistened in the sunshine. The men looked bold and handsome, their bodies smeared with clay and lion fat, while all wore feathers in their hair. It was a grand display.

Soon the clapping and the dancing began, and the competitors took their places. Matong, too, was there on his big black ox – but no one knew him in the feathers and the finery that had been provided by the magic skin. At least he *thought* that no one knew him! But Madikonyana's eyes were sharpened by her love for him, and her heart beat fast as she saw her beloved pass the winning post ahead of all the others.

Then came the leaping of the trench – the biggest test of all – and the crowd held their breath as the pick of the country's oxen came forward to show their strength and skill. But one by one they came to grief, until only the big black ox was left. Proudly he bore his rider to the hazard; then up, and *over*, he cleared it in a mighty leap, with his jet black tail streaming out behind!

Loud were the shouts and cheers that greeted this success – but Matong shyly turned his steed before the crowd had time to discover who he was and, riding back to fetch the chief's cattle home, he left them wondering.

That night, as he sat quietly beside the fire with the others, listening to the gossip of the day, the chief called across to him, "Matong, you missed a grand event today. Mai! What a contest between the brave and bold. What a pity that you were not here to see it!"

"But, Father," his daughter Madikonyana broke in when the chief had finished speaking, "Matong *was* here. It was *he* who won the two events!"

"Nonsense, my child!" the chief scolded the girl impatiently. "What silly talk is this? *Here* is Matong, the orphan youth who tends my flocks and herds. Tomorrow the victorious one will come to claim you as his bride." And she hung her head submissively.

On the following morning Matong took the cattle to graze as usual; but when he returned that evening, he was dressed in all the splendour and bold trappings of the previous day, and he rode home proudly upon the big black ox.

"See, my daughter," the chief called across the yard to where Madikonyana stamped mealies for her father's hut, "*this* is the man who has won your hand!"

"Yes, my father," she replied demurely, "but *still* it is Matong!"

Only then was the youth recognised, and his disguise seen through – and he readily admitted that it was *he* who had ridden the big black ox to victory on the previous day.

The chief was disappointed to think that his lovely daughter's hand had been won by a poor orphan boy, but he kept his word and allowed the preparations for the marriage to begin. However, he had no cause for regret in the years that followed because, apart from the bride-price of ten magnificent cattle provided by the magic skin, it also made provision for the community's needs for evermore.

Narrator: Olebagan Matlanyane.